LIGHT THE FIRE WITHIN YOU

Ida Greene, Ph.D.

Light The Fire Within You. Copyright © April 15, 1991; P. S. I. Publishers, 2910 Baily Ave. San Diego, CA 92105. Second edition October 1, 1996. Third edition May 12, 2004. Fourth Edition January 7, 2007. All rights reserved. No part of this publication may be reproduced, distributed, transmitted, transcribed, stored in a retrieval system, or translated into any language without the express prior agreement and written permission of the publisher. A portion of book sales is donated to Our Place Center of Self-Esteem, to help end violence

ISBN 1-881165-01-9

ATTENTION COLLEGES AND UNIVERSITIES, CORPORATIONS, AND PROFESSIONAL ORGANIZATIONS: Quantity discounts are available on bulk purchases of this book for educational training purposes, fund raising, or gift giving. For information contact: **P. S. I. Publishers, 2910 Baily Ave. San Diego, CA 92105 (619) 262-9951.**

Since the first publication of this book, April 14,1991. Ida Greene, Ph.D., RN, Marriage, Family, Child Counselor has established a non profit organization called, Our Place Center Of Self-Esteem, which assists children, and families coping with issues of abuse. A portion of the sale of each book is donated to **Our Place Center of Self-Esteem**. Dr. Ida Greene speaks; conduct seminars, and training on negotiation, personal and professional growth topics, (619) 262-9951.

Other books by the author are:
Self-Esteem The Essence of You — Are You Ready For Success?,
Soft Power Skills, Women and Negotiation™,
How to Be A Success In Business,
How To Improve Self-Esteem In The African American Child;
How To Improve Self-Esteem In Any Child;
Money, How to Get It, How to Keep It;
Say Goodbye to Your Smallness, Say Hello to Your Greatness;
Anger Management Skills for Children;
Anger Management Skills for Men;
Anger Management Skills for Women,
Stirring Up the African American Spirit and Angels Among us, Earth Angels.

ACKNOWLEDGMENTS

I wish to thank the following:

My father, for encouraging me to speak up and express myself. My mother for showing me her fears, so that I might not fall victim to the fears that enslaved her, because fear destroys faith. And faith is the key, that opens the door to the Christ Presence, "Kingdom Of God Within You." This inner power is the only power we possess.

So I thank God for implanting within me a spirit of power, courage, and a sound mind. Since the first publication of this book, April 14,1991.

Ida Greene

Introduction

Light means enlightment or understanding and truth. Light gives off warmth, and the warmth of this light is love. God is love; God is the warm light that breaks through darkness, fear, negativity, hatred, low self-esteem, anger, envy, greed, self doubt, uncertainty, and poverty. This loving light breaks through a lack of: money, loss, limitation, loneliness, misunderstanding, and unfulfilled relationships. Of the above feelings and emotional states, fear is the deadliest. Fear blocks our trust in God, lack of faith in yourself or God. Fears paralyze the mind and every cell in the body. It blocks out the natural light that exists in every cell in the body. When this happens, we feel isolated, abandoned and alone. The emotional states of uncertainty, doubt, distrust, worry, frustration, anxiety, anger, condemnation and fear, all prevent us from moving forward in life.

If we could rid ourselves of our rigid beliefs about life and the conditions we encounter, the above emotions could never affect us in a way to create havoc in our life. All of the negative emotions and feelings you are experiencing right now are deeply imbedded into the matrix of every cell in your body and mind. Therefore, if you desire to change the events in your life, or move in a new direction, you will need focus, clarity of purpose, self discipline and spiritual awareness. All of these will help you to release prior destructive mental and toxic emotional behavior patterns.

In this book we will address the emotional states of doubt, distrust, worry, frustration, anxiety, condemnation, anger, and fear. These emotions rob you of your self-worth, self-esteem and self-confidence. Most of the emphasis in this book will focus on fear, because fear has the ability to paralyze your thought processes, and render them useless to process new information. Fear blocks your ability to objectively assess your beliefs. It robs you of energy (drive), excitement (fire), and enthusiasm (light).

In my short life span, I have conquered a fear of: losing a job, buying a home, starting a new job, being a new wife, being a director of a large nursing facility, growing old, living alone, a fear of death, not having enough money, not finding a husband, a fear of being an "old maid", a fear of marriage, losing my independence, losing a child's love, being without a child, not being accepted, not being loved, fear of being rejected by my married friends after my divorce, fear of being a new mother, being a single parent, fear of swimming, skiing, fear of wealth, failure, success, public speaking, fear of mathematics, complex or mechanical things, a fear of computers, fear of writing a book, establishing a non profit organization, Our Place Center of Self-Esteem to end abuse and violence. We are looking for persons to be friend of the center by sending a monthly charitable donation to help carry on the program and activities of the center. If you have a question about violence regarding yourself, please e-mail me at idagreene@idagreene.com We also provide coaching and counseling by phone.

There are many fears that will render us helpless if we do not take control of them. Other fears I have over come are: Fear of writing a grant proposal, fear of losing a job, fear of an inability to meet my financial obligations, fear of re-entering the nursing profession as a registry nurse; fear of being made a "Do Not Return nurse to local Hospitals," fear of criticism, fear of commitment, fear that God would not provide for my needs, fear I would not find work when I was incompetent in my nursing skills by two hospitals, fear that I could not survive without a job/employer, fear of being alone, fear of growing old, and fear of being fat and unattractive.

I now know that God created all things, including the people in charge of them. I now place my trust in God, not people. Because anything people, or the world gives you, can be taken away. God is not like humans. If God gives you something and it is taken away, always expect an equal or greater good to replace what was lost or taken away.

God will speak intuitively to one of his human, earth angels, who will help replenish all that you lost with plenty to spare. Please do not attempt this if your faith in God to supply your needs is weak. Because if you do not see instant results, you might think this does not work, or that God does not care about your needs. Faith in will give you the patience and endurance to hang on until you see results. A weakness of faith is like a broken leg that is not strong enough to sustain your body. A weak faith will fail you. You will get angry, blame God for abandoning you and distance yourself from Him. You only need faith the size of a mustard seed to results. However, a little faith is better than no faith at all.

You only need a little faith to know that God is all you need. However, even a small amount of faith will fail you if your thoughts are rooted in fear. God is not a God of fear. God is a God of love. "There is no fear in love, but perfect love cast out fear." (1 John 4:18) It is easy to get caught up in the negativity you see around you and allow fear to dominate your thinking. Fear blots out the light in your body, cells, and life.

When we are consumed by darkness both within and without, light can not enter our body. You must eradicate worry, doubt, indecision, procrastination, apathy, and failure to act, because all of these are the precursors of fear. Of all the emotions we possess, fear is the most damaging to our self-worth, self-esteem, courage, ability to act, ability to risk, ability to change and cope with change, ability to handle adversity, ability to face rejection, ability to handle failure, and our ability to cope with loss of any kind.

When you gain mastery over your fears, you light the fire within you, to have energy, excitement, enthusiasm, joy, contentment, peace, happiness, aliveness, and love.

CONTENTS

Chapter 1

FEAR, THE FERTILE SOIL FOR STRESS

Recent surveys indicate that employees are taking a lot of things home from work today; anger, frustration, and tension. All are factors that produce a stress reaction in the body. All of these stressors are the result of fear, either real or imagined. Other fear producing stressors are: the reduction in work force, downsizing of corporations, technological advances that create a need for fewer people to perform job tasks, global and cultural reform, economic uncertainties, decreased need for manual labor, a growing tendency to devalue human beings, and a lack of appreciation for the contribution the *common* person adds to society.

Most people are afflicted with anxiety in some form. Others are consumed with feelings of uncertainty about the future. Many others have allowed their energy and aliveness to be drained by a deep fear of the unknown. They cannot live in the present moment because their mind is either in the past, dealing with unfinished business from yesterday, or with business that is in the future and is yet to come. They worry and fret about what tomorrow will bring. Then when tomorrow comes, they are so exhausted from the fears of yesterday and tomorrow that there is little energy left to deal with today's problems. You may be saying to yourself right now, I am not afraid of anything. Yet if we explored this matter further, we would find that you fear: growing old, being broke, cancer, AIDS, ill health, financial ruin, being alone, rejection, you will not be accepted by significant others, you may not get a raise on your job, what will

1

happen if you are fired from your job, being stopped by the police, having surgery, loneliness, the loss of love, death, speaking in public, you may not get what you want, being criticized, things may not turn out the way you envision, failure, bankruptcy, being audited by the IRS, and on and on. You can add other fears I did not list.

Much of the fear in society is rooted in changing times, and conditions. We are a materialistic people. We also are creatures of habit who become fearful, and anxious when there is uncertainty about our economic status, or doubt about our ability to provide for our livelihood. Change is one of the few constants in life. It is a constant that has been passed on to us throughout the generations of mankind. You would think we would have mastered it by now. But the truth is, that we do not handle change well. Change is an unknown constant; it is not a known factor. Because we are rational, logical, beings, it is unnerving to deal with an unknown constant. In fact, it can be very stressful for some people and unmanageable for others. Due to these factors, we must accept the fact that all of us may experience symptoms of stress at some point in our life. If we have developed effective ways to cope and manage stress, we are less likely to get a toxic build up of physiological chemicals in our body. The key is to be in touch with your feelings/ emotions to understand the interrelationship between the body, mind (thoughts), and emotions/feelings.

The emotions and feeling states that create the greatest challenge for us are: fear, worry, anger, rage, envy, jealousy, revenge, rejection, loneliness, sadness, disappointment, hopelessness, helplessness, and anxiety. All create a state of heightened readiness, and anticipation which causes a stress reaction in the body.

Stress is a nonspecific response of the body to any demand, be it physiological, psychological, or spiritual. Every high energy charge or demand we make upon the body causes stress in the body. It matters not whether it is in the brain, stomach, muscles, bones, or emotions. It is not what happens to us in life, but how we perceive what happens to us that produces stress in the body. It is the words you internally say to yourself that determine how you cope with life stressors. Your external view of the situations you encounter in life bears a direct correlation to your internal interpretation of the event.

Our body's chemistry is altered by the way we interpret the events that occur in our daily lives. A negative interpretation of events can elevate the corticotrophin hormone (adrenocorticotropin, cortisol) levels in your body, increase cortisol levels, suppresses your immune system, increase cholesterol levels, disturb digestion, cause an imprinting of the event in your memory, cause insomnia or sleep disturbance. The immune system is the body's first line of defense to fight, or ward off, invading bacteria into the body. Anytime the body is exposed to a stressor, or the brain interprets an event as a stressor, the following progression of physiological responses occur in the nervous system.

The nervous system, is composed of the central nervous system (brain and spinal cord) and the autonomic (automatic) nervous system. The autonomic nervous system, comprises the parasympathetic and sympathetic nervous systems. The sympathetic nervous system speeds the heart rate, constricts the blood vessels and raises the blood pressure. While the parasympathetic nervous system slows the heart rate, increase intestinal and glandular activity (thyroid gland, adrenal gland-urination), gonads (sex glands), and sweating. The illustration below shows how a perception of fear can act as a stimulus (stressor) to generate a hormonal/ physiological stress response in the body. The diagram shows how some may interpret a stressor. Be aware that anything another person says to you during this, will be based on their prior experience, of how they might react if they were in a situation like yours.

THE PHYSIOLOGY OF STRESS
Interpretation of Stress

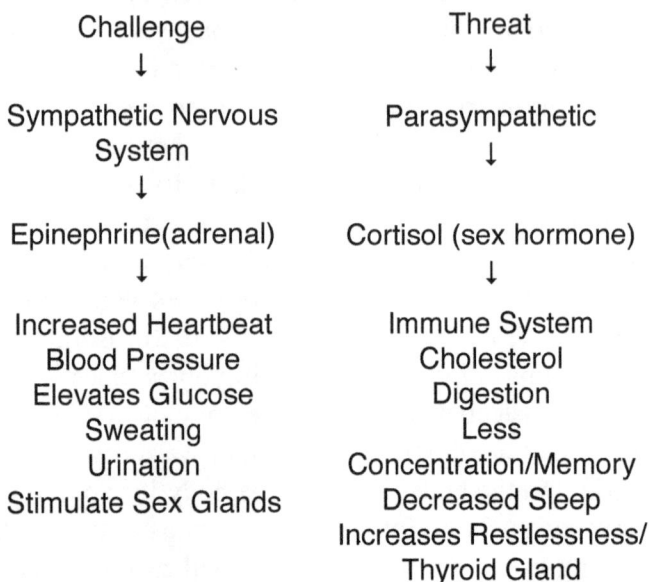

Challenge	Threat
↓	↓
Sympathetic Nervous System	Parasympathetic
↓	↓
Epinephrine(adrenal)	Cortisol (sex hormone)
↓	↓
Increased Heartbeat	Immune System
Blood Pressure	Cholesterol
Elevates Glucose	Digestion
Sweating	Less
Urination	Concentration/Memory
Stimulate Sex Glands	Decreased Sleep
	Increases Restlessness/
	Thyroid Gland

A study of the above diagram will help you to understand how a word or thought over a period of time can create a debilitating and life threatening condition in the body. Shakespeare said, "There is nothing good or bad, but thinking makes it so." The only meaning any event has in our lives, is the interpretation we give it. It matters not whether it is real or imagined. If we experience the events and situations as negative, and continually view them as threatening, conflicting, or fearful, we can expect to see permanent debilitating, destructive physiological changes in our body.

You can choose the way you look at and experience life. If things are not to your liking, you can rearrange your circumstances and implement changes into your life, more to your liking, in harmony with your life style.

You can see a bucket half empty or you can see it half full. Likewise, you can view the loss of a job as an opportunity to start a new career, or you can see it as the end of the road.

Our ability to cope with the stressors of life is directly proportional to the words we say to ourselves about the events that occur to us. For example, If you were laid off or terminated from work, you could say something like this to yourself; "I can develop a plan to deal with this situation," or if you are a spiritual person, you might say, " God has a better plan for my life and it is being revealed to me now."

Here are some things you can do to cope more effectively with stress or stressful situations:

First use a problem solving approach. To do this, you must **define the problem.** Why not try this now? Get a blank sheet of paper. Write out the problem/s you are now experiencing, in as much detail as possible.

Second, analyze the problem. Break it down into smaller parts so that you can identify the problem.

Third, brainstorm by listing or writing down on a piece of paper all the possible solutions to the problem.

Fourth, tackle the problem as if you had a high expectation of a successful outcome.

Fifth, look at and accept all adequate or reasonable solutions. The solution does not need to be perfect or be the best one. Now evaluate each solution against a list of criteria that states the conditions you desire, then select the best one.

Sixth, persist until you find a solution. You may want or need to adopt a new approach, add new resources, change your strategy or schedule.

Lastly, begin to implement the program. Try out some things to see how they work. If things do not work out as you would like, go back through this process again.

Often, when we are confronted with a stressful situation, our ability to problem solve is ineffective, due to prior learned ways of perceiving and reacting to stressors. You may have learned or developed a distorted mental framework, whereby you fail to see the obvious due to your automatic thoughts or behaviors.

The painful experiences we encounter in life are growth producing, because they make us stretch beyond our comfort zone. Discomfort is a necessary part of "the good life" you seek. When you pray to God for something you desire, it is wise to pray in this manner. Ask God for persistence, determination, emotional stamina, patience to endure the dark moments in your life, faith to wait on God's divine timing, divine illumination to know when to act, when to be still, and when to go within for divine guidance. After you go into the silence to commune with God, say to yourself, I am healed of all negative stress about this matter. Then Let It Go.

Self-management is a do-it-yourself job. We cannot gain control of our outer world until we master our inner world. Our inner world is often torn with strife, dissension, and unrest. I call this inner turmoil "the demon within us," for it tends to surface at the most inappropriate and inconvenient times. This "demon within" may take the form of stress, anxiety, fear, confusion, frustration, impatience, worry, anticipation, power, control, resentment, jealousy, envy, greed, or hatred. The demon, fear, seems to be ingrained within our collective unconscious psyche, (the collective race mind of all).

Within our inner world, the emotion of fear, is the most difficult to eradicate or modify. It can be destructive to our body, mind, and soul, if not managed properly. There is good in fear. It alerts us to impending dangerous situations. How ever, when fear is allowed to go beyond its limited useful boundaries, it becomes all-pervasive, all-consuming, and destructive. Fear must be managed at all times to best serve us. For it impedes the development of *trust and faith,* both essential character traits for the evolvement of our individual, emotional, and spiritual growth.

Form or manifestation always follow energy. Therefore, our greatest intention is always acted upon. Our intention, or intent, creates an anticipatory set of behaviors based on prior learned behavioral patterns. They allow us the opportunity to move forward with our plans, to create, and manifest what we desire.

If your fear level is low to moderate, you can create what you desire. When your fear level is high, you become immobilized with apprehension and anxiety, due to prior misconceived data, or false imaginings of your mind. Fear is a behavioral response in the body brought about by a physiologically real or imagined threat to the maintenance or the status quo of the physiological, emotional, or mental systems.

The earliest recorded mention of fear is in the Holy Bible, Numbers 14:26-28. "Then the Lord saith to Moses and Aaron, How long will these wicked people complain about me. For I have heard all that they have been saying. Tell them, the Lord vows to do to you what you have feared." They feared that God would leave them in the wilderness to die and it came about. This was a wrong use of fear by the Israelites.

Medical science now says that every single emotion we feel has an impact on some part of our body. Fear produces muscular tension, an over abundance of hydrochloric acid in the stomach, constriction of arteries, hypertension, muscular aches, over-tiredness, and a seemingly unending list of ailments. Emotionally, fear drives people away from us, makes us "needy," desperate, and lonely. making us angry, "uptight," and insecure.

What is fear? How do we get it? Where does it come from? Does everyone experience fear? Fear is an irra-

7

tional belief about a thing, idea, or event that seems real to the observer, even in the face of reality, which indicates that there is no logical observable basis for the fear. At the root of all fear is a thought form that was perceived in error, which on a previous occasion was associated with an activity that had no prior frame of reference to draw upon. The outcome was uncertain, thereby creating a situation of panic because the subconscious mind did not know how to handle the situation. The subconscious mind is the controller and manipulator of events in our inner and outer world. When the subconscious mind finds itself in unfamiliar terrain, it will attempt to escape from the situation to spare us embarrassment, or avoid having to figure out the matter.

The Subconscious mind is not a risk taker. It functions mainly as a computer to store and catalog the events and situations in our life. It has a corresponding behavioral template (back up system) for every activity we have encountered in the past. It works on an automatic relay of a behavior response system.

Whenever the conscious mind is given a challenge or presented with a situation, our subconscious mind has in its memory bank all of the behavioral reactions that occurred in the past, and it immediately relays them through a nerve impulse, and the behavior is manifested. We may experience, for example, tightness in the shoulders, constriction in the stomach, shaky knees, sweaty palms, or whatever bodily response our body has exhibited in the past. When we are faced with a stressor, we may notice and experience one or a combination of the above physiological responses or we may experience an entirely different reaction.

If we are in touch with our emotions, and desire to change the way we react to the people, situations, and events in our lives, we can choose to respond differently and create a new neuronal pathway and a new behavioral response. However, if we exhibit a new behavioral response to an old behavioral pattern it means that there is and has been a conscious effort on our part to input new data into the memory bank of our mind and to delete or neutralize the prior mental neuronal input. In order for us to experience a change in behavior; we must consciously input new behavioral data into our memory bank.

Thoughts are things and our state of consciousness produces its corresponding behavior. What we see in the outer world is a mirror of our inner thought patterns. All there is in the universe is energy. Fear begins as an idea or thought seed in our consciousness. Just as a seed, if nourished with energy, right nutrients and soil, will grow, to sprout into a plant or flower; so it is with a fear thought.

When a fear thought seedling is planted in the subconscious mind, given energy (ideal nutrient for growth and survival), it grows to become large and powerful. Each time we act out a fear response, and respond in a fearful manner, we add more energy to the original idea/fear pattern. The more energy a fear thought gets, the larger it becomes, until it becomes labeled anxiety.

Eventually, the constant repetition of fear reinforcing stimuli causes the fear thought form to enlarge until it consumes and controls our behavioral responses. Then it is called free floating anxiety. In this form, the person does not have to think fearful thoughts anymore. The fear stimulus has now become cued to many random behavioral responses, and any stimulus that closely resembles the original fear thought form will elicit the fear response in the body.

To eradicate fear from your conscious mind, you must not entertain fear thoughts through worry or doubt. Fear thoughts are very powerful. You only need to listen to another person express doubt or fear in your presence to activate your old programmed mental fear tapes previously recorded in your mind. When this happens, the experience becomes alive and real to you, as if it was occurring in the present moment. We are energy fields, states of consciousness; therefore, if we listen to another person express fear and we are sympathetic to their cause, it can affect us. The vibrations of their energy field can spill over into yours, and make your emotional field a part of their emotional field.

You must always stand guard at the door of your consciousness (mind), so that you allow only what is good and beneficial for you to enter your life. Remember, we all have our individual energy fields (states of consciousness); however, there is the collective mind/consciousness where all energy thoughts come together. Jung referred to this as the collective unconscious or race thought. These are the beliefs held by the majority of people. An example of this is, that most Americans believe in democracy.

If your energy field has a weak link, it becomes a part of whatever energy field is present. If your thought form does not have a strong electromagnetic charge (strong belief) which is greater than the opposing thought's electromagnetic field, it will not repel the energy charge of the opposing thought.

If the electrical energy field of your thought has a lower energy charge, it will take on characteristics of the thought form of the other person, be it fear or whatever. It operates this way continuously for all thought forms. This principle is seen in the Tony Robbins seminars. This is not to imply a right or wrong concept, but to suggest that we are influenced by the more dominant thoughts surrounding us. It may be to your benefit, or it may not. This thought process can be deadly for a juvenile, or an uncultivated mind trying to establish a self-identity.

Thoughts are living, breathing, things. They can and will evoke behavior, corresponding to the "mind set" where they are found. This is how we allow others to play with, manipulate, brainwash, or control our minds, and influence our behavior.

A person's lack of familiarity in a new environment may produce a fear reaction in the body. Since there is no past frame of reference or associate pairing of event to a situation, a new fear thought form may develop. The less fear response we display in a situation, the less fear we exhibit. When fears are deeply rooted, professional therapy may be needed to remove them.

Systematic desensitization is a treatment modality that works well with deep seated fears such as phobias. It works by defusing the energy charge of the old behavioral pattern. It uses a behavior modification paradigm whereby the old behavioral thought pattern is cued to a neutral stimulus, and through the process of selective stimulation, the emotional sensitivity of the behavior is weakened and thereby deleted from the behavioral repertoire. Fear is fertile soil for stress to grow.

Both fear and faith are identical, in that the energy used in the one is the same energy as that used in the other. Both are a thought and identical in their mental action. **Fear** is a *positive acceptance you will experience that which you **dislike***. **Faith** is a *positive acceptance you will experience that which you **like***. Fear is a mental attitude, so it can be converted to faith through your imagination or mental expectation.

You do not need to live up to anyone's expectations but your own. All of us are here by divine appointment and we each have a different reason and mission for being on the planet. It is different from anyone else. No one is in a position to judge you but God. And God does not judge us. You were given free choice when you arrived on earth to work out the best plan of action to help you achieve your state of Divinity.

You are not a failure. You have not failed anyone except yourself. Are you willing to assume responsibility for your decisions and behavior? The easiest way to solve any problem is to give the responsibility to someone else. However, when we do this, we lose, because we lose the opportunity to employ our decision making skills. Any skill we perform on a continual basis gets better with practice, including decision making.

Usually we are harsh, judgmental, and critical of ourselves. The best way to be accountable for your behavior is to become your best friend. Notice what kind of thoughts you say to yourself. Are they loving and supportive or self destructive words? If you notice that you are self-critical, begin to treat yourself with gentleness, kindness and patience. To love another person, you must first love yourself. Jesus said, God's Second Commandment was to love your fellow man as yourself. Our impatience and intolerance of uncertainty often force us to look for an easy answer to our problems. **Affirm to yourself**:

I am patient, for I know God always answers my prayers. I now place my faith and trust in God.

I am illumined, open to receive an answer to my prob - lem/s. I let go all concern about the "when" or "how."

I do the best I can, as I wait patiently for divine illu - mination.

Isaiah 26:3 states, *Thou dost keep them in perfect peace whose mind is stayed on thee"*

HOW MANY TIMES

How many times do we think that the road is too rocky
 for us to tread?
How many times do we long for the paths, That are

flowery and smooth instead?
How many times till we understand, That the load God
gives us is light; if it's shouldered with faith that He
knows the way.
And that morning will dawn out of night.
How many times do we have to learn, that he's there
every step of the way, and that He will guide us, and
all that He asks, Is just that we trust Him and pray?
How many times as we stumble and fall, on the way in
our upward climb, Does He reach down and lift us in
patience and in love?
Time...after time...after time. LEE SIMMONS

If You Have A Problem
If you have a problem that bothers you inside and time
does little to assure you that it will subside, Strip away
the fantasies, the negatives, the doubt, then draw upon
your inner strength and formulate a plan; and every
time you think you can't remember that you can.

Listen to your deepest voice where reason still
remains, and take control of your own life to minimize
the strains

Communicate your feelings so that you are not
alone.

A pattern of improvement in the change that you'll
be winning, If you'll just let a single step become a new
beginning. BRUCE B. WILMER

Chapter 2

LIGHT THE FIRE WITHIN YOU
MOVE THROUGH YOUR FEARS

Much of what our society teaches us is about the personality, the human part of us, which is referred to as the Id, (the primitive unrefined part of us, the Ego, (conscious reasoning part of us) and the Super Ego (exterior adjustment factor of guilt, which enables us to get along with others. Many persons, stop at this point and conclude that these three terms explain who we are, our motives, what we will do, or what we are likely to do. This explanation alone is inadequate to describe who we are, what we can do, or who/what we can become.

There is another part of us that psychology, sociology, and theorists do not address because it cannot be observed, quantified, or easily explained. This other part of us is the Spiritual self. The Spiritual self has two layers. It is both our inner most Divine Christ self, and our outer Spiritual protective layer, commonly referred to as Guardian Angels, Spiritual Guides, Intuition, or Sixth sense. These are the parts of our Self Identity, they are:

1. The Personality
    a. Id; b. Ego; c. Super Ego
2. Human Self
    a. Social; b. Emotional; c. Financial;
    d. Personal; e. Professional
3. Spiritual Self
    a. Holy Spirit; b. Guardian Angels;
    c. Guides; d. Intuition; e. Sixth Sense

Of the three aspects of our self, the Spiritual is the least developed. Neither psychology, sociology, or theorists address this part of our nature. Yet it is the only part of us that can synthesize all the other parts of our human nature. The spiritual part of us is the least understood and the part that we devote less time and energy to develop or improve.

There are three impurities and toxins that will block and stunt our spiritual growth. They are emotions of fear, envy, jealousy, greed, unrestrained anger; which will become hate if unchecked and deep seated feelings of unworthiness. The underlying cause of these feelings is a sense that we are separate from God, have a sinful nature, unworthy and undeserving of God's mercy and grace. God is with us. However, we seem to feel abandoned and left alone in the world to fend for ourselves. God has not left us. It is we who have abandoned God.

Our separation from God causes us to fear anything our mind can imagine, because we are mental beings. To cope with the complexities of life requires tremendous faith in an entity we cannot see, touch or feel. Faith cannot survive in the presence of fear. The precursor of fear is doubt. Doubt creates worry, worry creates anxiety, and anxiety create feelings of: helplessness, hopelessness, despair, futility, depression, unhappiness, lack of peace, lack of contentment, lack of prosperity and abundance, feelings of suicide, aggression, violence, destruction of self and mankind.

Because fear is the most potent toxin and poison of the body and mind. This book will address ways to overcome fear. Fear is darkness and the absence of light. When we are afraid all the light (the creator of energy) in every cell of the body is blocked and unable to be released from the cells of the body. So we have darkness from within. Every cell in our body needs to emit light, the precursor of energy, to keep us in a state of balance and health.

When we are fearful, all of the cells in our body shut

15

down and nothing can enter or leave the cells of the body. When this happens, the body is deprived of the vital nutrients it needs to maintain in a state of equilibrium. In this state of imbalance, we are an easy prey for the body to develop disease and for the cells of the body to decay and die.

Fear is a fertile medium for the development of diseases of the body, mind, and soul. Whenever fear walks in the front door, faith runs out the other door. Faith gets away as fast as it can, because it knows fear will snuff out its life and destroy it. Fear is the enemy of love, joy, happiness, peace, contentment, and faith. And where there is no faith, there is no spiritual development. And where there is no spiritual development, there is no God. And where there is no God, we feel abandoned, unloved, unwanted, and alone.

When we are loved we get a warm glow of light about us and we feel a sensation of warmth and love. When we are full of light, the darkness disappears from our body, mind, and soul (spirit). The brighter the light within us, the greater is the fire. Our fire gives us the energy and drive we need to accomplish our daily tasks. The light and rue inside us is waiting to get out, to radiate throughout our body and throughout the universe. What we send out returns back to us. To feel the light and love of our Christ self, we need to master fear .We have to move through our fears to light the fire within us.

Our fears are the barriers that hold us back and keep us locked into nonproductive behaviors, activities, and relationships. When we experience thoughts of fear, everything in our world appears to be out of focus. The mental image sent out may be clear, but our mind picks up and distorts the image. As we move through our fears, we light the fire within us.

Babies have only two fears. The fear of falling and the fear of loud noises. All of our other fears come with knowledge or develop as a result of our experiences, from what we see and hear.

We are beings of light. We have a physical and spiritual body of light. At the center of each cell in our body is an area of light. So in reality, we are a body of light.

All disturbing emotions affect our body in a negative way. Whenever we experience emotions like: doubt, worry, frustration, distrust, anxiety, anger, condemnation, hatred, rage, and fear; the area of light in the cells of our body contracts and shuts off. This prevents the natural inflow and out-flow of vital cell nutrients needed to maintain the body's inner state of equilibrium. This chemical imbalance affects our immune system, defender against foreign bacteria entry .Then alien, opportunistic bacteria enter the body, disturb its normal homeostasis, to cause cellular break down, and occurrence of disease. We are physical, mental, spiritual beings. Therefore, the foods we eat, the thoughts we think and our inner spiritual state all intertwine to keep us in a state of wholeness and wellness.

Physiologically, fear can be measured and quantified as stress or disease in the body. Fear can alter our life style and life span. Fear is the precipitating factor that causes individuals and countries to go to war against each other. It is the basis of all bias, prejudice, discrimination, and isolationism. Fear is the underlying emotion when people commit violent acts of aggression against each other. Fear underlies neurotic, and psychotic emotional breakdowns in the personality .And it prevents the development of love, and intimacy in personal relationships.

There is an interrelationship between our emotions and our body. We need to understand that our world of experiences and bodily functions is part of the eternal divine flow of life. All negative emotions produce a toxin that is poisonous to our body's cells. Therefore, the negative emotions we hold about ourselves and others affect us on a deep cellular level. They can shorten our life span and negatively impact our quality of life.

When we are frightened or tearful, a torrent of powerful chemicals, adrenaline, and acetylcholine, are released from the cells of our body and mind, to paralyze, and render them useless to function as normal.

Our fears are the barriers that hold us back and keep us locked into nonproductive behaviors, activities, and relationships. When we experience thoughts of fear, everything in our mental world and emotional world is non-focused. Due to prior conditioning, the mental images sent to the mind are unclear and distorted.

As we move through our tears, we let go confusion, negativity, and all emotional trauma of the past. As you develop spiritually, you begin to feel your oneness with God. When you know you are one with God; your spiritual awareness helps you eliminate worry, doubt, anxiety, resentment, anger, envy, jealousy, revenge, greed, and fear. Then you feel an inner contentment, peace, harmony, joy, happiness, and love which ignite the fire within you. Why not do it now.

DO IT NOW

Until one is committed, there is hesitancy, the chance to draw back, always ineffectiveness.

Concerning all acts of initiative, there is one elementary truth the ignorance of which kills countless ideas and splendid plans: That the moment one definitely commits oneself, then providence moves too.

All sorts of things occur to help one that would never otherwise have occurred.

A whole stream of events issues from the decision, raising in one's favor all manner of unforeseen incidents and meetings and material assistance which no man could have dreamed would have come his way.

Whatever you can do, or dream you can, begin it.
Boldness has genius, power, and magic in it.
Begin it now GOETHE

The **fire within us is the spirit of God**, the *Christ Presence*. In this state of oneness, we experience a state of bliss that is beyond description. From the earliest of biblical times, it has been said about mankind, "Ye are the light of the world." This light that we possess is the power and presence of God within us, seeking to find an outward expression in and through our lives. When we accept, feel and know we are one with God we live and act like a child of God. We are alive with drive, enthusiasm, and a desire to live in the "here and now."

When we are aware of our fears, and have control over them, they are unable to control our life. When our fears control our actions and reactions, we become a captive prisoner, of our own doing. As you work through each fear you are liberated. You learn to let go and let God help you. You begin to know with an inner knowing and trust that you are not alone. Through your faith in God you are able to overcome your fears one at a time. Jesus said "perfect love casts out fear" 1 John 4:18.

Also, the Amplified Bible sets forth the well-known writings of John in this way: "There is no fear in love— dread does not exist, but full-grown (perfect) love turns fear out of door and expels every trace of terror within our mind." What a magnificent statement of the power of love. This is a powerful affirmation to use in this era, when the many faces of fear are everywhere.

Love is the one emotion that can keep you sane, and centered in what often appears to be an insane world. Love can see you through the most difficult times and support you in the midst of the most demanding challenges. You can move beyond any fear caused by human differences whether it be differences in race, creed, choice of lifestyle, national culture, or difference of opinion.

Through love you can overcome fear of illness, lack, or any other condition that causes you concern. None of us can master fear by ourselves, and we do not need to try. You are never alone. God is as near to you as your breath. All you need to do is make time in your busy schedule, still your body, mind, and go within to commune with your Christ presence, for the needed inner strength. When you turn your thoughts inward, to focus on the Christ spirit, you begin to feel the calm love of God. This feeling of peaceful calm will remind you, that there is nothing to fear but fear itself. You can live, feel secure, and be at peace every day when you know, beyond a doubt, that God loves you and will never abandon you.

Fear is a natural and necessary part of life. The emotion of fear, should be our servant, not our master. Our mind is powerful. Whatever we impress on the mind, it will create. When our mind is besieged by false imaginings that we do not want to occur, they will happen anyway because whatever we acknowledge, we give energy. Everything is created through our energy and attention (sustained focus). It matters not whether what we focus on is negative or positive. We bring forth everything from the non manifested lifeless form, through our ideas and desires to the manifested form of life. We always start with an idea or desire, provide it with sustained energy (the object that is manifested can be positive or negative) to create manifestation from the unformed raw matter to sizzling life and formed matter.

Anything that we give energy and continuous focus, whether positive or negative will be created. Our mind cannot tell the difference between what is real or unreal. Our mind is creative and only knows how to create.

We came from an intelligent life force that created the earth through its spoken word. We came from this life force; therefore we are a part of it. God created our fleshed form to serve as a vehicle to bring forth" HIS will. Most of us are blinded by negativity, malice, greed, dishonesty, resentment, jealousy, revenge, bitterness, anger, rage, feelings of unworthiness, deep shame, low self-respect, appreciation, insecurity, hopelessness, help-lessness, self-destruction, and we are enslaved through addiction to chemicals and people. It seems we are unaware of the divine spirit that dwells inside us, because we continue to create conditions and life experiences we do not want.

We need to acknowledge the divine presence that lives within us and give this force permission to take control over our body, mind, and affairs to bring about God's will. Then our life circumstances will change. God's will for our lives is of a higher order. Because God wants to bring forth HIS kingdom on earth in and through our lives, we need to be willing to surrender all control and power to God and say "not my will, but thy will be done through my body, life, and affairs. This is why Job stated, "What I feared has come upon me."

Whatever you fear, assuredly *will happen,* because this is what you have given energy. You give life to things through your energy, intention, and imagination (thoughts). Anything you give life through your energy, intention, and thought will be created and will become your reality. This is why you need to pay close attention to the thoughts you think. Avoid dwelling on thoughts that frighten, because you anguish, or grief. Any thought that scares you robs you of your aliveness and energy. When you are afraid you *live in the past or future,* not in the *now.*

Our body's energy can be likened to the energy of a fire. A fire generates heat, light, movement, and action. The *amount of fire/energy we have is in direct propor - tion to the passionate drive of our inner life force.* Our life's mission gives us a feeling of purpose and a path to follow in life. Our inner life force is determined by the energy vibrations of the cells in our body. The amount of fire/energy we radiate from the cells of our body is the result of our level of aliveness or excitement about living, our ability to cope with the challenges we confront each day. Most of the fears on which we dwell daily are negative, non productive energy depleting, rather than life giving, "light," energy sustainers.

Our fears rob us of energy, stamina and the drive we need to handle our tasks of daily living. A lack of energy can cause us to be lethargic, procrastinate, act indifferent, and behave in a depressed, down mood. We were created to enjoy life and the fruits of our labor; "For God hath not given us a spirit of fear, but of power, love, and a sound mind." We need courage to conquer our fears. *We were born with and possess a spirit of courage, not a spirit of timidity and fear.*

Our fears keep us in darkness and prevent us from letting our "light-energy" shine through. The fears that handicap us the most are: *Fear of change. fear of rejec - tion. fear of power. fear of success. fear of money .fear of failure. fear of responsibility .fear of criticism. fear of ill health/ old age. fear of death. fear of expression. fear of enjoying life. fear of the unknown (problems that may not occur) .fear of being happy.*

Fear of Change affects all of us. We are creatures of habit. We like consistency because it allows us to predict our actions and reactions to others. We assume and expect the same situations and habit patterns to occur and if they do not, we fret, worry, and think that something is wrong. When we live in the "now," we do not worry about what will happen tomorrow. Jesus said, "Today's problems are sufficient unto themselves." We can only live in the "now." When we are strong in the faith that

God will take care of our problems, we can live in the "now". Then we walk by faith unafraid of change, because we know we will have a good outcome. Fear of change can keep you trapped in a non-productive job, life style, and relationship. To overcome this fear you must develop an anticipation of good things happening to you. And be open to new experiences.

We achieve mastery through every fear or challenge we have, because we learn from our weaknesses as well as our strengths. For it is through our new experiences of change that we expand our awareness to grow emotionally, physically, and spiritually. Change is a constant and will always exist. It is healthy for us physically, emotionally and spiritually to have a positive attitude about change because change is as inevitable as death. Both death and change are factors over which we have no control. God created this universe and our bodies to be in a state of continuous change. Nothing is stagnant in the universe. All living particles and matter create, die, or decay then recreate again. We did not create this universe or our body; therefore, we have no control over either. God created both and God alone controls both.

The only things you have control over, that you can change are: your thoughts, beliefs, attitude, amount of food you eat, the amount of exercise and rest you give your body, amount of pollutants, and toxins you put into your body (nicotine, alcohol, sweets, fats).

You also have control over your degree of satisfaction in life; based on your career choice, friendship and extracurricular activities. Likewise, you have control over your degree of happiness determined by control over the following emotions: envy, .jealousy, anger, frustration, acts of violence (verbal, mental, physical abuse). Lastly, you have control over your degree of joy, love, contentment, peace, humility, harmony, satisfaction with self and others based upon your spiritual maturity.

You will know you have reached spiritual maturity when you take God as your father/mother, and Jesus, or your higher power as your daily helpmate to guide you along the changing pathways of life. Those pathways may be strewn with obstacles, uncertainty, deception, confusion, loneliness, fading physical beauty, feigned affections, involvement with self-aggrandized individuals who want to make your property their own, unstable finances, disloyal spouses or significant others, disobedient children, and unloving, self centered children, family members, friends, or people where you work.

You need to do your best in all situations. Also, you need wisdom and spiritual discernment, to know when to let go and let God have your burden. This is when you need to say "not my will, but thy will be done," in my body, life, and affairs. When we surrender our will to God, our dread and fear of change ends. Prayer is an effective tool when you use it correctly.

In effective prayer you know that there is no place for anything but good in your life. You do not contradict what you affirm or want to happen. You accept that the statements you are making or have made are the truth about you and that they absolutely, permanently uproot, and obliterate every negative condition, or situation to which you are addressing. Never let yourself be misled by outer appearances or limited by the thinking of others, because prayer works by faith. You have to think the thought, and visualize the outcome before it happens. Prayer operates through the unseen spiritual world. So the laws that control its manifestation are spiritual. Therefore, it is believing is seeing, rather than in the material world where seeing is believing.

Pray or state what you want, but detach yourself from a particular outcome, because what is for your highest good may have a different form, or appear in a disguised manner. Both the Prayer of Serenity and the Prayer of

Faith can provide reassurance and hope that you are never alone. In your darkest moment when all has abandoned you, know that God will never abandon or forsake you. With God you are never alone. For scriptural consolation memorize and say aloud to yourself the 1st and 23rd Psalm, then read Psalm 46.

SERENITY PRAYER

God grant me the serenity to accept the things I cannot change, courage to change the things I can change, and the wisdom to know the difference.

The Prayer of Faith

God is my help in every need; God does my every hunger feed; God walks beside me, guides my way Through every moment of the day. I now am wise, I now am true, Patient, kind, and loving, too. All things I am, can do, and be, Through Christ, the Truth that is in me.

God is my health, I can't be sick; God is my strength, unfailing quick; God is my all, I know no fear, Since God and love and Truth are here. HANNAH MORE KOHAUS

Fear of Rejection manifests as a distorted self-image. This occurs when we are not firmly grounded in our divine nature or identity of who we are. We are a "child of God," a divine, significant part of the universe. Just as the stars, moon, and sun, we have a right to be here. We were chosen by divine appointment to be here at this time, in this place. We can feel rejected if our parents do not show us love or accept us, because we have allowed ourselves to believe that our earthly parents are the center of the universe. God is the center of the universe, not your flesh mother or father. God is the one who gave you life, and God is the one who will take it away from you at the appointed time. No one, including your parents can keep you from dying, when God decides your earthly stay is completed. Your parents cannot create a body. They are the vehicle God chose to house your body and soul for nine months. We come through our parents' body, not from them. We were created by God. We came from God and when our stay on earth is over we return to God, not to our earth mothers and fathers.

We need to learn to let go of all earthly physical or emotional attachment so we are not in bondage to the physical plane when we depart. The physical universe is an illusionary state of being that we create through our imagination. It is temporal, short lived, will not, and cannot sustain us over long periods of time. However, the life we create through God and Jesus is secure and lasting.

This is the *only* relationship/love that is enduring, unchanging, and can sustain you throughout your earth's journey. The "Ten Commandments" state this boldly. It says "Thou shalt have no other Gods before me, for you will love one and hate the other." Gods' love for you and relationship with you will last through out eternity. Your relationship with your parents, children, spouse, lover, significant other, friend, grandchild, earth idol, hero, guru, is all short lived. They will eventually reach a point of decay and death. No one is able to give you the same emotional support as God. We all have our down moments. We humans tend to identify with each other. So your "down moment" may come at the same time as the person to whom you look for support. Then you feel let down, abandoned, and hurt. All human relationships are here to serve you. They are temporary, not lasting. They can never, and will never, equal the love, security, joy, peace, or understanding you find in your relationship with God.

God is the only person that will never abandon or leave you. Often we go to God angry, disappointed, and exasperated because we did not receive from another human being what we expected. All human beings are incomplete. We are all at different stages of our Christ maturity. Your reason to be in a human body is to perfect your physical, emotional, social, and spiritual self to attain your Christhood. You cannot compare yourself with another person. Nor should you look to them for the answers to your problems. Others can suggest, but they cannot tell you how to live your life. Each of us marches to a different drummer, and only God know the lessons we must learn to reach our Christ state. God wants you to lean on Him completely as you learn to stand on your own spiritual feet, so you bond to "It/Him alone." I use the term It here and throughout the book to remind you that God can not be equated with your earthly parent. God will not change toward you because you do something that He/It does not like. God is changeless.

Your parents were given the privilege of nourishing, and bringing you to adulthood, at which time they were to let go so that God could bring you to spiritual maturity, and awaken your mind to wisdom and divine illumination. Everyone has issues with their parents about things they didn't do, things they felt they should have done, or a particular relationship that did not meet their needs or expectation.

No human will ever be able to love you with the depth and intensity that God does. What you long for and often seek in the physical realm is a feeling of contentment, security, and bliss that can only be satisfied in your relationship with God. God wants to use our relationships with other members of the human race to refine, mold us, and tame our emotions and self destructive tendencies so we are pleasing and amenable to allow "It/Him" to work through us, to bring about Its kingdom on earth.

Your parents will never be able to love you with the depth and intensity as God does. Your parents may not have known how to show their love or caring if they did not receive love and caring from their parents. It is impossible for you to give to another, what you did not get as a child. As we begin to focus our attention on God, we develop unconditional love for ourselves and for our fellow man. Everyone, parent, children, spouse, lover, significant other, friend, grandchild, earth idol, hero, guru-needs enough self-esteem and spiritual discernment to step aside, get out of the way, to let God take you through the pathways and over the rugged roads of life, so you get the necessary refinement and spiritual fine tuning you need to achieve mastery and attain Christhood. It matters not, that you feel you will never measure up to be exactly like Jesus. That is all right. You have a role model to emulate. Jesus is non partial and does not have favorites. Jesus said that "the rain falls on the just and unjust alike." And if you should be of a religious doctrine that sees Jesus as a wise or learned person, that is all right.

Everything originated from God and all will return to God. There is no religious persuasion, doctrine, or creed that can keep you from going through the experience of death. You may be an agnostic, atheist, famous, a bum on skid row, rich, poor, learned in your field of study, a prostitute, ex-prisoner, devoted husband, loyal wife, or obedient child. None will get off planet Earth alive. *Everyone will go through the experience called death.* Each of us will give an account of what we did, or did not do, with our life during our stay on earth. You are here by divine appointment. You were allowed to come here because both you and your Father/Mother/God thought you could make a positive contribution to mankind. Do you know why you were sent to earth? Why do you exist, to do what, for whom, under what circumstances? This is your mission.

We all were created by God and sent to earth to be of

service to mankind, and to do the will of God. Not your will. We are to let God's will be done in our life and through our body. It may be that your mission on earth is to give pleasure and enjoyment to your parents, family, and friends for one hour, one day, one year, or seven years. My foster son's stay on earth was 15 years. For two unmarried young ladies I knew, one, a cousin, lived to age 26, and my godchild lived to age 29. You must never question God about death or ask why death had to occur at a given time. A contract is made between you and God before you come to earth, stating how long you will be on earth, and what you were sent to do. Maybe you have forgotten the purpose or mission for which you were sent to earth.

Most of us get so absorbed in our emotions, and activities that we have little time to become quiet, still our mind to allow God to commune with us. God will never force Himself upon you. Before you came into this experience called life, you were given free choice. You have the power to choose what you will do, when you will do it, with whom, and for whom you will carry out your mission to be of service to God. You were created by God to bring about His divine mission on earth for all mankind. You are the vessel God uses to reach out to humanity. God needs to use your eyes, hands, ears, nose, mouth, intellect, mind, smile, sensitivity, gentleness, your skills to speak to impart wisdom and knowledge, and your skill to use the written word to formulate concepts in a coherent manner so that God's wisdom and teachings are passed from generation to generation.

Someone made a statement to me that the words written in the bible by the prophets have been sealed and is not to be tampered with. I do not have a problem with that. I feel that God will and does use any medium consecrated to Him, whose purpose for existence is to do God's will, to bring forth "HIS" kingdom on earth. Now that I have given you a gentle nudge, do you know why God created you? Your mission might be to impart the word of God, the love of God, the patience of God, or to share God's understanding and compassion through your outreach ministry.

We are all here on the planet to serve God and be of service to mankind. This is the primary reason all human beings exist. We were made in the image and likeness of God. You belong to God. You are here primarily to carry out God's mission to create harmonious relationships between all races and nationalities. And secondly, to be united to each other.

All of us originated from one source, God. God does not, cannot, and will not be fragmented. We are all brothers and sisters. Whatever affects the one, affects the many. If you stub your toe, do you not feel the sensation of discomfort in other parts of your body? Of course you do. Likewise, if a member of the family of mankind hurts; we feel the hurt as well. This is why we reach out in love and compassion to help each other in times of misfortune.

You left your ethereal home to come to earth to help mankind to unite as one family, the family of God. We said, "Here I am, Lord, send me," and you were sent to earth to bring forth God's mission. You have forgotten that you were sent to earth by God, to share your gifts and talents as only you can do. You were not sent to be a self centered consumer. You were sent to give Inspiration, Motivation, Hope, Love, and Joy. You were sent to be a peacemaker, to promote harmonious relations between people, to share your bread and goods with those less fortunate than yourself, to allow God to use your mouth and gifts of expression to impart "HIS" wisdom to your brothers and sisters who have gone astray and forgotten their divine heritage. You are here to help your lost sisters, and brothers who have forgotten the way home. You

30

can be the beacon of light to show them the way back to the compassionate, forgiving, loving arms of God. God will never reject you. Jesus, as well as your Higher Power, stands ready to assist you.

The Father will never force "Itself" upon you. You have to be willing to follow the path of Jesus, role model, and way shower. You must willingly say, "Here I am Lord, send me." "Not my will Lord, but let your will be done through my body and life." We are part of the family of God. All of humanity is our family. So we need never fear rejection. Remember, no one can reject you without your permission.

The road of life is often rugged; but the presence of God in you, is greater than any force outside you. You only need to call upon God to get needed help. If you feel apart from God, know that God is not the one who has moved. God is nearer to you than your breath. However, God has given you free will. God will never force "HIMSELF" upon you. You have to be willing to give up control over your life and invite God in to mend the broken pieces. With God by your side, you can survive the valleys of despair. Try this now. Sit quietly, go within your mind. Ask Jesus or your Higher Power to show you how to feel oneness. Bring to mind a problem you are going through, or have gone through. See God making your path straight, and the road no longer rugged.

THE RUGGED ROADS OF LIFE

Life is an ever increasing spiral on the path to human perfection. It matters not the hue of your skin; the color of your eyes, nor the color of your hair.

Self mastery is an inner process that happens each time you overcome an obstacle. No one can ever deter - mine, the depth of your learning experience.

So continue on your journey to overcome your stiffest challenge, For no one will ever know, the depths of your overcoming. Continue to strive for excellence in everything you do. For the path to fulfill - ment and happiness is the rugged roads of life. IDA GREENE

Fear of Power is often seen as a weakness or lack of courage. We may either fear the power of others or, by acting from our irrational perception of what we believe is power, cause harm to those around us. Often, we are afraid of the perceived power of the other person. When we fear someone t s perceived power, we revert back to our parent authority figures and behave in a childlike manner. We are afraid to speak up on our behalf, so we bury our feelings of frustration, anger, and rage inside of us.

Power can be experienced as Hard or Soft Power. *Hard power is an outward behavior of aggressive acts or action when we interact with others based on our irrational fears.* Most of us are acquainted with the use of "hard power" because it is woven into the matrix of societal values. It is a byproduct from the pioneer settler days in the United States of America. The power struc- ture then employed aggression and force to conquer land and subjects. From this structure emerged the behaviors of toughness, intimidation, aggression, force, dominance, and ruler ship. It was common and acceptable to attack if threatened with a loss of power or of bodily harm. We use "Hard Power" when we bulldoze through a negotiation, using force, intimidation, and scare tactics to obtain our objective. When we use force, intimidation, or aggres- sion in our business encounters, we tacitly legitimize the use of hard power. Hard power uses physical, mental, or emotional force rather than people skills.

Soft Power takes a humanistic approach to power. Humanism is a way of looking at our world. Humanism emphasizes the importance of human beings, their nature, and their place in the universe. Humanism teaches that every person has dignity and worth and therefore should command the respect of every other person. God created us in "HIS" image and likeness; therefore we have value and are valuable each unto itself. There are no greater or lesser persons except in our mind; in our mental perception of power and the importance we bestow upon people. To avoid comparing yourself to others, seek to mentally see the presence of God in yourself and in all people. The presence of God is in all people, whether or not we or they acknowledge it. As we recognize the power and presence of God in ourselves, and others we gain a perspective of power that excludes no one.

Fear of Success — To achieve success, we must believe that success can happen, that it can happen for anyone, and that it will happen for us. Most of our energy is used in a destructive manner to dwell on what we fear may happen. Our mind creates through our mental impressions. It will create whatever our mental energy presents to it. If our thoughts are focused on what we fear may happen, or on what we fear may never happen, our mind will create it. Your fears are borne from the dark imagining in your mind thinking of what could possibly occur. To avoid getting into the habit of a fear reaction, still your mind, focus on *what could be,* rather than on what is taking place in your life now. Just know that God wants you to reach your goals. Your dreams are the divine thought seeds planted in your mind by God to help you have a larger experience of your divinity. The infinite intelligence of God needs you as an expression of "HIMSELF" Know that all of life wants you to be a success.

Often your fear of being successful may have its origin in one of the following areas: 1. To exceed family members or family expectations of success 2. Non-acceptance by the individual and parent/s of appropriate behavior to expect from the successful individual 3. Fear that one's (parents) may reject them because the parent fears the child may reject those 4. The parent/s may feel uncomfortable relating to the successful child due to their feelings of inferiority or inadequacy.

Our fears are the barriers that hold us back and keep us locked into nonproductive behaviors, activities, and relationships. When we experience thoughts of fear, everything world appears to be out of focus. The mental image sent out may be clear, but our mind picks up and distorts the image. *As we move through our fears, we light the fire within us.*

Any of the following feelings may affect your performance: feelings of unworthiness, undeserving, poor judgment, and helplessness, a need to belong or identify with a group. This is a good exercise to learn how to cope with these feelings. Write the answers to the following questions in the book now.

1. "What am I doing or saying to myself, that makes me think I do not deserve more good or something better?"

2. Make a list of feelings you have felt today.

What are you feelings right now, besides discomfort, tightness of shoulders, shallow breathing?

3. Go over this list daily, and place a "+" next to any feeling or feeling state you notice. To enhance your objectiv-

ity, pretend you are doing this exercise for a friend who has told you they want to know the truth about themselves. What do you notice? A feeling I notice about myself today is:

Feeling/s I Notice About Myself Today

M	T	W	TH	F

1. Feelings of unworthiness
2. Feelings of undeserving
3. Low self-esteem/lack of trust
4. Lack/low self-confidence
5. Laziness/procrastination
6. Helpless/desire to be cared for
7. I lack trust in decision making

Failure and success are two ends of one stick. Thoughts of lack manifest as limitations, and thoughts of abundance manifest as happiness and success. Jesus said "...anything you pray for asking and believing, you will receive and it will be done unto you ".When we place our attention on the Christ presence within us, we know that God wants only the best outcome for us. When we believe and accept this premise, our energies can be constructively utilized because we are willing to serve God through our service to mankind. The following poetry can help you learn to expect a better outcome.

ALWAYS REMEMBER
Remember to forget the things that made you sad, But never forget to remember the things that made you glad.
ELBERT HUBBARD

WHEN FACED WITH A MOUNTAIN

When faced with a mountain, I will not quit,
I will keep on striving, Until I climb over,
Find a pass through, tunnel underneath or stay and
Turn the mountain into a gold mine With God's help

ROBERT SCHULLER

To personalize this poem insert <u>me or my</u>

THIS IS THE YEAR

Wonderful, Wonderful, fortunate you (me),
This is the year that your (my) *dreams come true!*
This is the year that your ship comes in;
This is the year you find Christ within.
This is the year you are glad to live;
This is the year you have much to give.
This is the year when you know the truth;
This is the year when you find new youth.
This is the year that brings happiness;
This is the year you will live to bless.
Wonderful, wonderful, fortunate you,
This is the year that your dreams come true.

RUSSEL A. KEMP

Fear of Money manifests as *lack and limitation*. Because we fear having money, we may act irresponsibly; squander or misuse it. We must respect money, for it has an energy vibration of its own. Money will not remain where it is not respected and appreciated. Also, you cannot hold negative thoughts about money or the people who possess it. ***God made everything good, including money***. Money is not bad; it is the love (worship) of money that gives us trouble. You cannot make a god out of money. Money is a necessary commodity to purchase goods and supplies for our daily needs. However, we must employ self-discipline and use good judgment as we accumulate and dispense money. Do not try to hold onto or hoard money. Money is energy, and energy circulates continually. It is never stagnant.

The amount of money you have for your use is based on your self-esteem, which is based on the belief that you are one of a kind, created in the image and likeness of a loving, perfect God. It is done unto you as you believe. What you mentally see is what you will produce. Jesus stated, "If ye have faith as a grain of mustard seed, ye shall say unto this mountain, remove hence to yonder place, and it shall move, and nothing shall be impossible to you." Most of us do not have a positive belief in goodness, justice, and right action. This causes us to be enslaved to our fears, worries, and doubts about our livelihood.

Faith is a positive belief in what we want to experience, and fear is a negative belief in what we do not want to experience. Both are states of belief. Our mind can not occupy two states of an opposing belief at a time. We will either believe in a positive outcome (faith) about money and money substance, or we will think on and visualize a negative outcome about money. Our belief about money is based on our learned irrational fears. Use the following strategies to help you develop a prosperity consciousness.

1. Develop an inner knowing of your divine and unlimited potential. Accept God as your willing partner to provide all your needs. This will require faith and belief in a power that cannot be seen through the physical eye. Jesus said, "All things are possible to him that believeth." Mark: 23. Do you have this faith?

2. Ask yourself what is your divine purpose for being on earth? All human beings were created to produce and prosper. Life is a reciprocal process. It is about giving and receiving. When you can clearly understand how prosperity benefits your life's purpose to survive on the planet, it will unfold naturally for you.

3. Define with clarity why you want to be prosperous. What is it that you would love to be, do, or have? What is it you desire to manifest into your experience that would benefit you while enriching the life of your fellow man? Do you want more money to provide security and material pleasures for your loved ones? Write down your desires right now on paper. Be specific and give descriptive details of why you need the money, and what you will do with the money once you get it.

4. How will you having money benefit mankind? Allow your imagination to soar and imagine how your life would change positively if you had this money. We really can have all we desire. But having it all means more than material wealth, career success, or loving relationships. We will need to grow spiritually to develop an unshakable faith in God before we can have all we desire. For it will require that we develop patience, a tolerance for ambiguity, change, a letting go of control, so that you are able to listen to the quiet and still voice of God as it dictates the direction and path you must take to have what you desire.

Affirmation

1. *Quiet and grateful, I am attuned to the steady, dependable rhythm of the stars and the orbiting heavenly bodies of the celestial universe.*

2 *I am safe and secure in the dependability of the Kingdom of Heaven.*

3. *Life, love, harmony, and peace reigns supreme within me.*

Conquer your fear of lack and limitation. Some people experience the crippling fear of "not having" with greater intensity than they experience the power and exhilaration of having. Limitation is what most of us have been taught to accept as normal. "Do you have difficulty feeling what it would be like to be rich? Do you need to unlearn negative programming or false beliefs about money? You can do this through daily meditation, visualization and affirmation. Ask yourself, "What fears are preventing me from getting what I want in life?" Jesus said, "Fear not, little flock, for it is your Father's good pleasure to give you the kingdom." (Luke 12:32) God wants us to have our heart's desire. But it requires that we have a trusting, and loving relationship with God. This means that you will need to cleanse your mind of negative ideas about God's ability to handle your problems. Write you thoughts about this below.

This cleansing process can force you to change your fears into the positive energy of enthusiasm or determination. You must deny the reality of any appearances that seem real. If you think about what you do not want to happen one minute, and the next about what you want to create, your mind will create both. The mind cannot tell the difference between what is real and what is imaginary. Also, you cannot embrace another person's reality as being true for you. What may be true for them will not be true for you.

Take a pragmatic approach to obtain your good by creating a plan of action. It is already your divine right to have what you desire. We need to assist the universe to deliver our daily supply to us. We must take action to help attract into our life what we desire. We need a fearless belief, determination, directed focus, and a plan of action to assist God to supply us with the good we desire. What is your plan of action?

Develop a daily habit of meditation, affirmation, and visualization. Meditation is a way to open the door of your subconscious mind to love, beauty, and insights that dwell inside you. After you become centered to focus through your daily meditation time, a verbal recitation of key affirmations can be a powerful tool to help saturate your mind to bring forth what you desire. The use of affirmations can also help to bring forth your life's purpose and to enhance your spiritual growth.

A general prosperity affirmation Kerry Reynolds Ph.D. recites is — "God is all there is and I am part of this infinite Presence. God's natural abundance is always mine to have; it is the only security I need. I live in an energy of unlimited potential and so it is. "This affirmation stated specifically what he wanted to bring forth. After stating your affirmation, you must be able to visualize it. Your mental picture must clearly delineate what you desire, it must be believable and seem achievable to you. *To create something from invisible to visible, you must believe it, see it, and vividly experience it with your senses, until it manifests for you.*

Become open to the joy of giving. When good is lovingly and unconditionally sent out to the universe, it returns tenfold. If you are uncomfortable with giving, start giving until it feels good to you. We can find ways to tithe everyday in small ways. You can send an unexpected $100 to a struggling student, leave an extra tip for a harried waitress, give a hug to someone who needs it, praise someone who appears discouraged, or compliment a person who seems insecure. Remember to keep the energy of love and prosperity flowing in your mind at all times. What will you do?

Build and maintain a prosperity consciousness. Prosperity is not a five-step process to be exercised thirty minutes a day. Prosperity is a way of life; to be lived each day with exhilaration, anticipation, and passion. For *the thoughts we think, directly affect the way we feel.* The language we use is powerful. Especially the nonverbal words we repeat to ourselves more than a hundred times a day. You must think and speak prosperity daily to feel it, and for it to manifest in your life.

Give thanks to God for the blessings of life. The greatest gift we can give to ourselves is to maintain an attitude of gratitude to God for the past good we have received. Being grateful allows us to humble ourselves before God and it gives us reassurance that we are not alone. When we are thankful, we are thinking upward and positive, rather downward and negative. It is difficult to be thankful and negative at the same time.

Learn to love the experience of life. Love all of life, the painful challenges as well as the pleasurable moments. Live life with joy; then more joy will be created in your life.

PROMISE YOURSELF

Promise Yourself to be so strong that nothing can dis - turb your peace of mind. To talk health, happiness, and prosperity to every person you meet.

To make all your friends feel that there is something in them.

To look at the sunny side of everything and make your optimism come true.

To think only of the best, to work only for the best and expect only the best.

To be just as enthusiastic about the success of others as you are about your own success.

To forget the mistakes of the past and press on to the greater achievements of the future.

To wear a cheerful countenance at all times and give every living creature you meet a smile.

To give so much time to the improvement of yourself that you have no time to criticize others.

To be too large for worry, too noble for anger, too strong for fear, and too happy to permit the presence of trouble. CHRISTINA D. LARSON

HOLD FAST
Hold fast to dreams
for if dreams die,
life is a broken winged bird
that cannot fly.
   LANGSTON HUGHES

Prosperity Promises From the Bible
Beloved, I wish above all things that thou may prosper
and be in good health, even as thou soul prosper.
(John 111:2)

Surely goodness and mercy shall follow me all the days
of my life... (Psalm 23:6)

No good thing will he withhold from them that walk
uprightly. (Psalm 84: 11)

The Lord shall increase you more and more, you and
your children. (Psalm 115:41)

Fear thou not; for I am with thee: be not dismayed;
for I am thy God: I will strengthen thee; yea, I will
help thee; I will uphold thee with the right hand of my
righteousness. Isaiah 41:10

Fear of Failure is an expectation and concentration on
what we don't want to happen; fearing the worst brings it
about. Failure is a state of mind that is created through
our imagination; therefore, it is a relative and subjective
state.
   To create anything new requires you to change your
behavior. Change is not easy for any of us. Usually we
resist change because we are unable to project our desire
into the future, to see a positive outcome. All growth-
mental, emotional and spiritual-requires that we let go of

42

old beliefs and habits. Jesus said that we could not put new wine into an old bottle. Likewise, we cannot create new behavior from an old behavioral pattern. For the new behavior will be contaminated by the old. To make lasting changes in the creation of a new behavior entails that you let go of the old to make room for the new behavior. This is also true if you want to make a positive change in your lifestyle. *We need to let go of the old to make room for the new.*

Fear of Responsibility can take the form of helplessness, being or acting like a victim, emotional/mental blocking, or an unwillingness to act on our own behalf. Our spiritual growth may require that we experience pain, as well as pleasure, along life's way. Each of us has a different spiritual path to follow because our emotional weaknesses and character development are not the same. Some of us may need to grow in patience, while others may need to learn to be honest in business transactions, overcome greed, envy, or jealousy. The spiritual path of growth will be different for each of us. Therefore it is unwise to mimic or follow the lead of another.

We are all on an individual spiritual journey through life. Our spiritual path may intersect that of many people; however, that does not mean we must or should walk in their footsteps. Each of us must carve out the divine road map that lies before us. No one can travel the road of life for us, even though it might be an act of unselfish love. We each must meet God face to face, to be aware of the powerful presence that controls the universe and allows us to enjoy the fruits of life (joy, peace, contentment, happiness, and bliss).

When we come to the realization that we can never own the universe because it is owned by God, we will be able to relax and enjoy the splendor and wonders of planet Earth. When we are relaxed, we are able to do all the things within our capability, to create a higher quality of life for ourselves and others. But we must let go of our control, to let God rule the universe. We are a co-creator with God, not the Creator. To accept this enables us to relax and enjoy the journey of life.

We will all depart earth through death. However the life force that is God is unchanging and lives forever. It cannot die or be destroyed. It can only recreate itself in the form of new life, which we call human beings. Once we learn the rules by which life and the universe operate, we can work within the confines of our human potential, to achieve a state of at "Onement" with God. This is the beginning of wisdom and spiritual awareness.

Life is a revolving door. It is eternal and can never die. It can only recreate itself in the form of another human life form. And as one soul grows and prepares for its departure from planet earth, another soul enters, through the birth process, to learn its special lessons for its soul evolvement in the attainment of the Christ life. And the cycle continues through God's divine plan of creation and recreation. I believe this is what Jesus was referring to when he talked about life eternal.

A Fear of Criticism will often prevent you from expressing yourself as a unique beings, because you have failed to establish boundaries of who you are; what you like and dislike. Therefore, we are constantly looking outside of ourselves to discover who or what we are. We do not have a strong, positive, inner image of ourselves; therefore we are unsure and emotionally fragile. So we constantly seek validation and approval from others.

Because we look for validation outside of us for approval and acceptance, when others do not accept us or disagree with us, we become unsettled or fall apart. When we do this, we become a carbon copy of everyone we meet, and just another face in the crowd. Then it becomes impossible to discover where we begin and where others leave off. A fear of criticism can also cause us to have low or no self-confidence. The beauty of our soul is radiant and its effect reaches far beyond the number of people we meet daily.

Fear of Old Age/Ill Health can cause us to worry and live in the future; dreading each day, unable to grow old gracefully. It is a fact of life that our soul is eternal and that the cells in our bodies age gradually. The aging process can be altered through positive and affirmative thoughts. However, aging occurs because we live in a society that believes and supports a concept of decline of the body and mind after age 65. God is a spirit and has eternal life. When we identify with and become one with the spirit of God, we take on the character traits of God. Then our countenance and attitude remains eternally youthful. It is better for us to develop a Christ countenance and attitude than to focus on our physical beauty. Because our flesh is a manifestation of the race beliefs (aging and deterioration) of the society in which we live.

THAT WHICH LIES WITHIN US
What lies behind us and what lies before us are
tiny matters compared to what lies within us.
RALPH WALDO EMERSON

A **Fear** of **Death** is a refusal to live. It is certain that we will have bad times, disappointments, sadness, sorrow, and challenges in life. But none of these is a reason for us to fold unto ourselves or close off our heart and mind to life and living. In the bible it states, "Man was born to trouble. "To be human means that we will have human problems. The only people who do not have problems are the dead. We came into this experience called life, to work on the flaws in our character so that we might become more like Christ. We are destined to be great and to enjoy the fruits of the spirit. However this can only be accomplished if we set our sights on the Christ life and seek to become more like the Christ each day.

The Christ life is one of service to God and mankind. When we take on the Christ mind, we listen to, respond to, and follow a higher calling. We are in continual prayer and meditation as we say "not my will, but let thy will be done through my body and in my life" Then give up trying to control or manage your life. Be alert to listen to the voice within us as God directs your life.

You were created in the image and likeness of God. It is therefore your mission and obligation to evolve physically, spiritually, and emotionally to your highest and best self. Dying is easy. Anyone can swallow a bottle of pills or put a gun to their head and pull the trigger. It takes courage to live in the face of adversity, or when all around you is in total chaos and your world seems to be falling apart. Discouragement is a luxury you cannot afford. You just need enough faith to believe in God's promise to you "that HE will never leave you alone nor abandon you." This brings to mind a poem by James Dillet Freeman entitled, "I Am There."

I Am There

Do you need me? I am there.
You cannot see Me, yet I am the light you see by.
You cannot hear Me, yet I speak through your voice.
You cannot feel Me, yet I am the power at work
    in your hands.
I am at work, though you do not understand My ways.
I am at work, though you do not recognize My works.
I am not strange visions. I am not mysteries.
Only in absolute stillness, beyond self, can you know Me
    as I am, and then but as a feeling and a faith.
Yet I am there. Yet I hear. Yet I answer.
When you need Me, I am there.
Even if you deny Me, I am there.
Even when you feel most alone, I am there.

Even in your fears, I am there. Even in your pain,
  I am there.
I am there when you pray and when you do not pray.
1 am in you and you are in Me. Only in your mind can
  you feel separate from Me, for only in your mind are
  the mists of "yours" and "mine."
Yet only with your mind can you know Me and
  experience Me.
Empty your heart of empty fears.
When you get yourself out of the way I am there.
You can of yourself do nothing, but I can do all.
And I am in all.
Though you may not see the good, good is there,
  for I am there.
I am there because I have to be, because I am.
Only in me does the world have meaning; only out of
  Me does the world go forward. I am the law on
  which the movement of the stars and the growth of
  living cells are founded.
I am the love that is the law's fulfilling.
I am assurance. I am peace.
I am oneness. I am the law that you can live by.
I am the love that you can cling to.
I am your assurance. I am your peace.
I am one with you. I Am.
Though you fail to find Me, I do not fail you.
Though your faith in Me is unsure, My faith in
  you never wavers, because I know you, because
  I love you.
Beloved, I Am There.

JAMES DILLET FREEMAN

Quotations To Heal The Heart and Mind
Failure Doesn't Mean You Are A Failure...
It Means You Haven't Succeeded Yet.
Failure Doesn't Mean You've Been Disgraced

It Does Mean You Were Willing To Try.
Failure Doesn't Mean You Don't Have It...
It Does Mean You Must Try Harder.
Failure Doesn't Mean You Should Give Up
It Does Mean It Will Take A Little Longer.

ANON

AFFIRMATIONS

God is my source. My good is coming to me now!
Because God-life is at the center of my being, my mind
and body are continually healed and restored.
I relax and give thanks that God is my health.
God, I am grateful that your presence is always with me.
Good health is my natural state of being. Thank You,
Father, Mother, God. "
The reality of my divine inheritance is good health. It is
unchangeable.
There is no condition that I can contract that is beyond
God's power to heal. I am healthy, happy, and whole!
Praying for healing, I hold to thoughts of health. While
praying for prosperity, I count my blessings. My prayers
are answered at the right time, in the right way, all in
accordance with God's will of good for me.
All negativity is released from my consciousness. Human
conditions no longer pull me down. My faith and trust are
in God alone.
I am convinced that everything is always working togeth -
er for good. And so it is. I am not bound by the past. Each
day is a clean slate for me to write on. I let go the past,
to begin anew.
I devote time each day to become still, immersed in God's
presence and love. This feeling of oneness with God
renews my mind. I am open to see new good in my life.

"The eye is the lamp of the body. Therefore, if your eye

is sound, your whole body will be full of light." (II Matthew 6:22) It is essential in creating equality between men and women to be able to face our individual and collective fears as human beings. Women and men face fear differently. Women have learned, to share their feelings and that to reach out for support is acceptable. However, the contribution women make on a large scale is insignificant, as a result of being told over centuries, that their opinions did not make a difference, that is beginning to change today.

Some men are afraid to look inside themselves, because they fear what they might discover. For women to be treated as a spiritual equal to men will involve honesty and respect for the mystery that exists between the sexes; and love for the parts of each sex that cannot be understood. Individuals sometimes engage in partnerships; however, each sex must maintain its dignity and respect for the other sex. Words like "freedom, equality, and power" are recent additions to the definition of a woman. Since Roman times, these words were reserved for the definition of men, that is changing rapidly today.

The person who is a bringer of hope knows that believing is seeing and does not judge by appearance. The bringer of hope releases all fear and doubt. They know evil is an illusion. They listen to the voice within them, and know the truth about themselves. The person who is a bringer of hope acknowledges the good in all and empowers those around them. A person who is a bringer of hope understands the power of the mind and focus their thoughts on positive expectations. A bringer of hope rejects a consciousness of lack and celebrates abundance. They know there is no such thing as hopeless or impossible.

To obtain a state of inner peace, say to yourself, "All effort, pressure, and urgency are now dissolved from my mind and body. I am filled with peace as I envelope myself in God's embracing oneness". We must hold vigil and be continually aware of our thoughts, words, and actions. We need to live in the recognition of the "I AM" presence of God within us, and in the light of what we know to be true. We must become beholders and obedient to this Divine life force. As we grow in spiritual maturity, our attention will be directed toward what is real and what is absolute. And that which is unlike God will disappear from our life, for it will have no power or hold over us. During this inner change, begin to state daily, your inner verbal dialogue. And say, "from this moment on, I exercise dominion over my thoughts and inner awareness. My mind is now stayed on the spirit of God, as I behold all of life from this vantage point. I now banish all negative thought patterns and behavior from my consciousness. I am free from fear, anxiety, worry, and concern. I bask in the light of my spiritual awareness. All is well with my soul." Can you depend on yourself? Do you trust yourself? Are your motives and actions consistent so they can be relied upon? Being able to depend upon your ability to be consistent in all circumstances, and under all conditions is essential for self discipline and self mastery. Personal dominion is necessary in building a constructive, effective, balanced life.

Can other people depend upon you to be consistent, reliable and trustworthy? Do you keep your word to follow through on your commitments? If you can depend on yourself to do what you say you will do, you will be dependable in your personal relationships. If this is an area of weakness for you, start small. Start by keeping your commitment with insignificant matters and follow through on them. Your belief in yourself and in your competence will improve with each successful accomplishment. Remember, you are attempting to create a belief system (consciousness) out of nothing. So it is a matter of building a mind set or consciousness of dependability. You want to prove to yourself that you are trustworthy and can depend on yourself to follow through to support the goals you want to accomplish.

As we recognize our oneness with God, we are able to trust ourselves because we realize that we are not alone. The power and presence of God is closer to us than our breath; we only need to acknowledge God's presence and ask for assistance with matters that seem beyond our scope and comprehension. However, when we turn our problems over to God, we have to let go, so that God can work out a divine solution. God does not need our help and will not work with us jointly on a problem. Either we handle our problem/s or we turn it over to God for divine resolution. If we do the latter, we must have total faith and trust in God to resolve the matter for us. If we have any trace of uncertainty, or doubt about God's ability to find the perfect outcome, nothing will happen, until we depend upon God completely, by letting go and stop worrying.

The Bible teaches us not to react to events, but to act from the center of peace within our being. For what lies behind us and what lies before us are tiny matters compared to what lies within us. "That which is within you is greater than that which is in the world." The key to a balanced, effective life is to maintain peace and a feeling of quietness within us. Say to yourself, "The world will continue to spin but I do not need to spin with it." No matter how turbulent the storms of life may be, we need to find an unfettered place where we can go to still our mind, to communicate with the Divine impulse of life, I refer to as God.

At the center of all hurricanes, there is an "eye "where everything is calm and still. No matter how much activity and confusion may be around you, if you go to the stillness at the center of your being, you can find peace and strength. When you get control over your inner and outer world you will have dominion over every aspect of your life. Then no one can say or do anything to upset you. At the center of your "true self" there is calm, quiet, peace, and stillness. Deep within you is a center of peace, harmony, and balance. For it is there where your Christ spirit dwells. When we become still to know our inner Christ Presence, we are free from all distractions and confusion. For this is where you dwell in the "secret place" of your Higher Power. There is nothing but a Perfect God, perfect being, perfect woman, perfect man.

We must hold vigil over our thoughts, words, and actions so that we are aware of them. Our being of who we are, is in the recognition of the "1 AM" presence and power of God. We become beholders of like things, when we view all things in the Christ light of what we know to be God. All of our attention is directed toward what is real and absolute; that which is unlike God dissipates, for it has no substance, power, or hold over us. Mentally repeat the following statement: From this moment on, I exercise dominion over my awareness. My mind is stayed on the Divine. I behold all of life from this vantage point. Therefore, negative patterns of thought and behavior are banished from my mind. I am free from fear, anxiety, worry and concern, I bask in the light of my spiritual awareness; all is infinitely well with me. And so it is.

We suffer from spiritual amnesia, acting as if we are human beings having a spiritual experience. *We are spir - itual beings, who are having a human experience.* Spiritual insight is natural to us, if we take off the blinders of our conditioned thinking and belief. When we allow ourselves to shed our old way of being in the world, the real self can come forth and express itself. Once we have entertained a belief in lack and limitation, we cannot know abundance and prosperity, because lack and limitation are a disease of perception. Once there is recognition of wholeness and well-being, our low self-esteem is replaced with self-love and self-confidence.

Because we trust in the world of appearances, we some times panic, when things are not the way we think they should be. You must learn to trust in the perfect activity of God, which is always taking place. It is called spiritual discernment. This means looking beyond appearances, whether good or bad, to realize the truth about the matter. The truth is: There is only a perfect God, perfect man, perfect woman, and perfect child. There is order and perfection in God's world. All chaos, confusion, struggle, and disorder are created in your mind. Not God's mind. This is why you have to unify, or become one with God, to get a true picture of your circumstance. The freer you become, the less you are affected by situations in your life. Learn to stand steadfast in your spiritual awareness. Then everything works together for your good, because God is guiding your life and affairs.

See all negativity being released from your mind. Then your human conditions can no longer pull you down and influence your behavior. Repeat this affirmation to yourself right now. "My faith and trust are in God alone. I am convinced that everything is always working together for my good. And so it is. I am not bound by the past. Each day is a clean slate to write on. I let go of the past and begin anew. I devote time each day to become still, to become immersed in God's presence and love. This feeling of oneness with God renews my mind. I am open to receive my good." The eye is the lamp of the body. So, if your eye is spiritually well, your body will be full of light. Matthew 6:22

To face our individual and collective fears is essential to create equality between men and women, However, men and women face fear differently. Women, have learned that sharing feelings and reaching out for support is acceptable. They are able to look inside at their emotions and fears. However, women need to learn how to work through their emotions, so they are not imprisoned by them.

Affirm for yourself, *"From this moment on, I exercise dominion over my awareness. My mind is stayed on the Divine. I see all of life from this vantage point. Therefore, negative patterns of thoughts and behavior are banished from my consciousness. I am free from fear, anxiety, worry, and concern .I bask in the light of my spiritual awareness; and it keeps me functioning efficiently and effectively toward my full potential."*

Discipline is putting yourself in charge of yourself, of doing what you decide to do, of being what you decide to be. Discipline gives you control over your life and affairs. The practice of self discipline assures that all aspects of your being obey your will. Discipline over your habits, your thoughts, and actions is essential for making life an exciting enfoldment. When your mind is disciplined, everything falls in place in your life, because you determine what thoughts to think.

Discipline on all levels is important. Spiritual disciplines, like meditation and prayer—are especially significant for personal growth and spiritual enfoldment.

In disciplining yourself to maintain constant contact with God, you establish and maintain God's authority and dominion over all aspects of your life. The mind is disciplined to be a servant of the soul. We are spiritual beings as well as physical; therefore, we understand the benefits of living a disciplined life.

Sometimes when you have a lot of challenges to meet, it is easy to doubt your ability to meet them, so you feel alone. Yet if you keep on, you will not fail. Even in defeat, the Christ centered person is victorious, because you win the greatest victory of all, which is victory over yourself.

You are not alone. For you are one with the sustaining will of God. You are one with the order, the goodness, the heroic, and one with the triumphant spirit of life (God). To help strengthen this feeling within you affirm now, "Lord, I believe; help thou my unbelief. " Know that there is no cry that is not heard by God. And there is always an answer. There is a love and a power greater than the fears of dark imaginings of your mind. There is wisdom, and a way to do whatever you need. Let your heart hold to faith and belief in miracles. The way is made plain to you when you are in a relaxed state, open to receive with no judgment, or expectation of how things should be.

Humility includes many esteemed qualities, such as patience, modesty, simplicity, gratitude, and quietude. Humility is not weakness; it is the ultimate strength. As you humble yourself, you are not only closer to God, you become one with God. Express this now, by letting God's will flow through you without interference from any limitations of your personality. See your self free from all outer; or personal concerns, as your soul is absorbed in the Infinite. You are filled with awe as you give thanks for the abundance God gives you.

Affirm, "All effort, pressure, and urgency are dissolved from my mind and body. I am filled with peace as I am enveloped in God's Oneness. God's love transforms, heals, blesses, and uplifts me." Thank God that you have the innate capacity for expressing "HIS love. As you liberally express love, your relationships with others are harmonious, happy, and free.

Love is never critical or self righteous. God's love expresses itself through us frees us from the tendency to be impatient with other persons or to be unkind. God's love inspires us to see and appreciate the good in other persons. God's love expressing through us inspires us to be understanding, gentle, and unselfish in our dealings with other persons.

Coping with Difference — A fear of persons whose cultural background is different from our own. To overcome our deeply ingrained beliefs is the most difficult challenge in coping with persons of various cultural backgrounds. Many of us have had limited exposure to the cultural practices of other minority groups, and we cannot defeat our learned, negative reactions to people who seem different from us. If you have a fear of someone whose ethnicity is different from yours for example, African-American males, discuss your fear openly, either with another African-American male co-worker whom you know well, or with Anglo friends who have relationships with African-Americans. Ask them to tell you about their experiences with interracial personal and business relationships. Do this with the intention that you want to learn as much as possible about the other person's culture and positive attributes so that you confront your fears of the unknown to lower your anxiety level.

Remember, African-American individuals or members of any ethnic groups have the same desires and motivation of all people. They are in the same gathering as you for the following reasons: to obtain knowledge, to advance their career or learn ways to advance their careers, and to enlarge their circle of social contacts. If you cannot accept that, and if you don't have acquaintances who can offer insights into your feelings, I would suggest talking to a counselor.

Many people feel discomfort in the presence of persons who are different from them. As the work force changes, so must your irrational fears about other people. A part of your job as a human being is to take risks, to personally develop, and to culturally grow.

To mature means that you need to be open to new and varied people from all walks of life. Life is not easy. It was never meant to be. To be fully human means you are willing to grow through your fears, confusion, apprehensions, and emotional pain to experience peace, love, and tranquility, which is the absence of fear.

THE SERENITY PRAYER
God, grant me the serenity to accept the things I cannot change; the courage to change the things I can; and the wisdom to know the difference.

FOR RELIEF
Cast thy burden upon the lord, and he shall sustain thee. Psalms 55:24

FOR RELEASE
Let us do our work conscientiously and thoroughly and leave the results to that law, "God" which is perfect. — The Science of Mind, page 60

Releasing a problem can be like putting down a heavy burden. And if we're experiencing limitation or challenge with regard to our health, relationships, or finances, letting go of the burden is a welcome relief. The Science of Mind maintains that whatever we think about succeeds, so if we're succeeding at carrying a burden the obvious thing to do is to change our thinking.

Universal Mind is neither affected by nor concerned about pre-existing conditions, or the restrictions and confinements of the past, which is why we can always change the bad to good and the good to something better. Our part is to keep an affirmative vision. Our seed thought is what counts. We must nurture it and not revert to old patterns. If we do wander off-course, we can give thanks for the good now in our lives as well as the good we want in our lives. Then encouraging signs of a new direction will start to appear.

In Affirmative Prayer, Release is the fifth and final step. "Cast the burden" of all limiting conditions from our experience as we let go. We affirm right action and all good, releasing it to Spirit for the perfect manifestation.

Affirm Freedom

I claim my freedom now through the Christ spirit within me. No matter what the circumstances, true freedom can only come through the inner life and strength of Christ in each of us. Through the all-conquering power of Christ, we are free from any limitations. Let us acknowledge that Christ within us is a freeing, healing, forgiving presence. When we tap into the unlimited resource of our inner Christ, we no longer limit ourselves or our good. Through Christ within us, we are free.

Light The Fire Within You

Move from Fear to Faith (a positive belief), Conflict to Peace, Lack to Abundance, Sickness to Health, Despair to Hope, and Sadness to Joy.
  REV. IDA GREENE

Fear

This exercise will help you cope with fears of the unknown.
1. Write what you feel are your fears. Write them now:
A.

B.

C.

Now list ways you feel you can cope with these fears. Write out your answers below:
A.

B.

C.

To respect your fears, admit and acknowledge them to yourself. Write down how you can learn to respect your fears while you are working to eliminate them. All fears are not bad. It is wise to fear what would happen to you physically, emotionally, and spiritually if you used mind altering drugs or chemicals.
My Greatest Fears Are:
1.
2.
3.

Write below how you can respect your fears:
1.

2.

3.

Identify what bodily reactions you have when you experience your fear/s? Most fears are so powerful that you can have feelings of panic or anxiety due to past behavioral conditioning. If you need to close your eyes to mentally re-experience these feelings, do so. Remember to take in a deep breath of air, before you close your eyes. Then go ahead and allow yourself to mentally visualize your past fearful bodily reactions; write down what you remember or may be experiencing right now. Be willing to confront your fears. Admit that they are uncontrollable and that you are willing to work on managing them. What is the worst thing you imagine could happen if you allow yourself to feel these emotions of fear?

We all fear our inner self is so horrible that no one could possible love us. We also fear loneliness, failure, not being in control of things and the unknown. We love misery, and chaos. *We are most afraid of enjoying life, of having things workout to our advantage, and of being happy.*

Our lives can be likened to a theatrical production. It is a theatrical stage to refine and polish our character flaws. As we move through the veil of our inner longings, wishes, desires, insecurities and doubt, anxiety and fear, we emerge the polished gem that sparkles. And you show the way to those coming after you as you graduate from your earth experience

All Angels need an opportunity to grow and develop to their fullest. Earth is designed to polish and refine your character flaws so that you become perfect earth angels and attain your Christ perfection. You are here by divine appointment. What is your purpose and mission for this lifetime? What fears now block your Christ mind? Develop a plan of action to overcome this.

MY PLAN OF ACTION

A. Identify your Fears and possible causes. Go over this list of fears twice.

FEAR   **CAUSE**

B. Identify the origination or possible cause of your fear.

C. Do the next exercises to discover the causes of your fear.

How to Overcome Fears To Light The Fire Within
a. Identify feelings you have of low self-esteem:
b. What do you suspect to be the cause or origin of it.
c. State your reasons and be specific.
d. List three ideas or attitudes that reinforce your fears.
1.

2.

3.

Decide what you want to tell yourself to better understand the cause and truth underlying the above situation, event, action.

How to Cope With Fear
To discover the cause/s of your fear/s write the following:
Past fear — This fear is similar to an emotional, mental, or physical pain I experienced:
(a) What
(b) Who
(c) When
(d) Where

I need/want to act now, but I am afraid of:
(a) Retaliation
(b) Rejection
(c) Unknown
(d) Outcome
(e) Stirring up past
(f) Others angry at me
(g) Loss of love
(h) Procrastination

Move Through Fear, Overcome Stagnation, To Take Action

When you face your fears and uncover the mystique, dread or uncertainty of the outcome. Learn to accept and visualize a positive outcome. Get movement do something discuss, explore, or change your behavior, then confront your fears. Remember action cures fear, because your energy is no longer stagnant, you are less mentally paralyzed and able to act. You and your energy begin to flow and move.

How to Rid Yourself of Fears
Create a plan of possible approaches, or solutions.
Get a sheet of paper, or write in this book the following.
Put in your own details:

Pro = for	Con = against	Outcome
New house	Get loan Pack/unpack	Move

Chapter 3

THE ADJUSTMENT FACTOR

We need to create a space for people to move toward or away from us. We should never force ourselves into an environment that is closed, restrictive and unloving, because this creates an energy field for us to experience non-acceptance and unloving behavior.

During one of my meditations, I mentally stepped outside my body as if watching a television show of my life. I saw myself crouched in a corner, paralyzed with fear. I heard a voice speak to me through my thoughts and say to me, "Let go, you have all power in your hands." I reflected back upon my earlier years as a child and realized that I had given up my personal power because I wanted to be accepted and loved by others.

Acceptance was such an overriding emotion in my earlier years that I was hungry for acknowledgment. I wanted to feel like a worthwhile person. In my earliest childhood, I recall that I was not accepted by my mother because of my fair-skin coloring when I was born. In Minters, Alabama, where I was born, blacks and whites did not mix together racially and an indication of such resulted in the person being run out of town and possibly killed. It was rumored that I was fathered by a white man. There was much consternation and unsettling of emotions at the time of my birth. So much that my mother feared for my safety and left Minters, Alabama. She stated that she left Alabama and walked to Pensacola, Florida, with me in her arms at four months of age. It was there that I grew up and experienced childhood and young adult life. I was a fair-skinned child, due to the hereditary characteristics of my paternal great, great grandfather who was white.

My mother found it difficult to accept me. I did not resemble her, or my maternal grandparents, whose skin was very dark, and had true African features. This early experience of non-acceptance by my mother forced me to seek acceptance from my father. My father had a powerful mental field and tended to overshadow and dominate all who entered his energy vibration field.

As a child, I must have decided it would be to my advantage to please daddy and receive his love than to please Mama and not receive love. I gave and I received a tremendous amount of love from my dad. In my family, Daddy was the one with power to say "yes" or "no" Mamma usually deferred all matters to Daddy, unless he chose to include her. Daddy always had the final word. As a young child, it brought a smile to my father's face whenever I did as he instructed. I made very few decisions without consulting my father. If ever he disapproved of an idea I had, I immediately dropped it for fear I would lose his love or approval. My father became my God. My father was God to me and I was his little girl even at the age of 35, when he made his transition. I always lived in fear, wondering who would take care of me if Daddy should died. The thing I feared came to pass. I was totally devastated by my father's sudden, premature death.

I stayed in a state of shock for four months or longer. I did not want to let go of the one person who I felt loved me totally and unconditionally. I did not get to know God personally until my father died. I have often said that my father had to die so that I might live. After my father's death, I had to get to know God in a personal way, because I had idolized and worshipped my father. I never knew the proper relationship between a heavenly father and an earthly father. They have different powers and roles, but I did not know how to separate them.

I was fearful when my father died because I looked to him as the source of all my Good. I did not know about my own divinity .It was very hard to accept the constant urging of life telling me that I was divine, that I was one with God, that I did not need to fear because I would never be cut off from the source of my Good or love. I did not know about divine love.

When we acknowledge our divinity and oneness with God, we no longer experience fear, because we know we are one with the source of all Love and Good. We may not always know the why or the how but if we trust God, the way will be shown. And the right path will light up and brighten before us. If we have trust in God as the source of our supply and Good, we would know there is nothing to fear .It is only when we look outside ourselves, rather than within, that we lose our connection with the source of our Good, God.

We have to look deep within our hearts, for the secret of life, permanent .joy, and security .Faith is the key element to a life without fear; however, faith fades easily in the presence of doubt, anxiety, or fear .Faith is a faculty of the mind. It is a mental attitude so inwardly embodied that our mind can not deny it. There is a power (1 call God) that will work for us all, but it is up to each of us to have belief in it. As stated in the Bible, no obstacle is able to stand when a definite statement is made with deep feeling and faith in God or Jesus.

When we have an appreciation and thankful attitude for all the experiences of life, we invoke and increase our faith factor. We must work not only on our physical body, but work, as well, on our mental and spiritual bodies. For in so doing, our souls evolve to that of a Christ vibration. Jesus said, "Fear not, for behold, I stand at the door of your heart and if anyone acknowledges me and lets me in to commune with him/ her they have peace in their hearts and never want for their daily needs, for they have already been provided before they ask." God (I AM) is in tune with every spiritual energy vibration in the universe and responds at once, simultaneously, allover the world when anyone taps into this divine source of Good (There is great power in the words "I AM" the name of God). Trust is the answer to fear. Trust is faith. And Faith is the key to the kingdom of God, the source of all good.

Ask God for a belief that is unshakable that you know how to tap into divine wisdom when you encounter fearful situations. When there is harmony in your inner world of experiences, you will see a change in your outer world. God is in charge of the universe and knows how to run it. We only need to trust. We must set aside our free will and be open to God's will to experience the joy and beauty of a peaceful mind and world. I admit that it is not easy, but it is worth the price we would pay to be saddled with our unwanted fears. We are all sojourners on the same path to enlightenment. Our task is to know and experience our oneness with God, to master fear.

Learn Optimism

Learn Optimism vs. Pessimism says there is no hope; it's all your fault. Optimism says there is a way and I will find it.

- It is easy to be optimistic when things are going well.
- Our positive exploratory style affects our optimism.
- It is everyone's mandate to be successful.
- Success is when we have total balance in our lives.
- Self talk is how you speak to self when bad things happen
- Empathic communication: open your eyes to shift paradigms; to see through the eyes of others and put yourself in their place.

- Earn someone's trust; create rapport with the person so that he/she feels you are on his/her team.
- The power of your subconscious mind is the ability to control your stress.
- The power of positive optimism is the key to success and peace.

Your emotional bank account is like your check book, ask yourself, and "Is it full or over-drawn?" To increase your emotional reserves, remember to do one of the following for yourself and another person each day. *Give*:
1. **Praise**-Shower yourself and others with it.
2. **Encouragement**-Give and expect to receive.
3. **Keep a promise**-Let you word be your bond.
4. **Have Positive Expectations**
5. Say **I apologize**, when you have messed up.

Do one of the above each day for a week. Write your results below.
Monday –
Tuesday –
Wednesday –
Thursday –
Friday –
Saturday –
Sunday –

AFFIRMATIONS
Today and every day, I hold to the truth, I know, Regardless of the appearances, there is no condition in my life that can control me or keep me in bondage to it. Through the spirit of the Christ in me, I am free. I praise God for the strength to overcome habits that are not healthy or beneficial. I do not rely on other people or physical substance to achieve what I am already capable of achieving.

The Christ Spirit within enables me to rise above every challenge and to experience victory'. I am free with the freedom of the Spirit of God within me. I choose to live in a way that promotes personal growth and happiness: I think positive thoughts, I help others, and I spend time each day in prayer and meditation.

I give thanks for my freedom to think, to choose, to express, and to be the wonderful person I am. I praise God for this gift.

Affirmation
I do not mind waiting for others, nor do I mind waiting for things to happen. Perfect order and Divine right action prevail as I live on God's time and let everything flow forth from Him.

Chapter 4

FEAR, THE ENEMY OF REASON

Developing trust is easier said than done. I had a deeply entrenched mistrust of men from early childhood that I have had to work on diligently to eliminate from my consciousness. On occasion, I can still detect traces of this trait. As a little girl, I watched my father become involved in an extra-marital affair. He took me everywhere he went, even to his girlfriend I s house. I resented the fact that he had a girlfriend, that he would let me see her and that he was cheating on my mother. Since I thought of myself as his favorite person, I did not want to take second place to anyone, except my own mom, for his affections. I told my mom about his rendezvous, and that ended my outings with Dad. Sadly, it did not end his extra-marital affair. I decided then, at age five, that men could not be trusted and, since God was a man, I was not sure if I could trust Him with my feelings.

It is amazing how the mind reasons at age five, but I was hurt and crushed beyond words. Now I know that God is not a man, and does not behave this way. I have accepted God as a Universal Spirit that has both masculine and feminine aspects. This has helped me to get rid of my distrusting feelings towards the masculine gender. I was afraid to trust men. I now also know and accept that God does not think or behave as we humans think and behave. God's behavior or reactions cannot be equated to those of us humans. We are rookies who are blindly stumbling along the path of life unaware that we need to move up in our consciousness (thinking) from our human self to our Christ-self. We need to move to the Christ mind set and gentleness of Jesus. However, the sad state of affairs is that we have programmed gentleness out of the behavioral repertoire for men. Men are told to be strong, tough, and hold back on showing their feelings. However, when we look at the Holy Bible, we notice that Jesus was a very gentle, compassionate, and loving man. Yet he showed strength and power.

By today's standards, Jesus would probably be labeled effeminate and possibly homosexual because he had a group of men (his disciples) following him. If He had kissed Judas on the cheek in today's world, he would have been labeled gay.

How is it that the man who displayed feminine characteristics in his dealings with others was the epitome of gentleness, kindness, understanding, compassion, and love, revered by all Christians, leaving a living testimony of how men and women should treat each other. A large percentage of men in our society has ignored the perfect male role model of all time. Jesus is not the exception. He is the example for us to follow. It takes great self discipline when someone strikes you on one cheek to turn your other cheek and let them slap you on it. It is challenging to not be offended when others say mean and malicious things about you. And to say Father, forgive them, for they know not what they do. All people know on an intellectual level, but they lack understanding on a spiritual level.

The key is for us to not react on a human level with retaliation, but to forgive seventy times seven. This is why I want to live to be 100 years old. It takes time to achieve personal growth, emotional maturity and spiritual maturity .I notice an improvement in my spiritual growth every year, and you will too, if you make this a top priority. Never get to the place where you think you have it made in the area of spiritual growth and maturity. We keep learning and improving until we take our last breath.

I now agree with the wise sage who said that life is a theatrical stage where we act out our life experiences. I say life is a school, where you never stop learning. For just when you think you have it made, life presents another lesson to be learned through a greater challenge. Therefore, I have decided that if there is such a thing as reincarnation, I do not plan to come back to planet Earth again. I plan to learn all the lessons presented to me in this life and get the right spiritual understanding so I won't have to repeat any lessons. All spiritual lessons are wrought with pain because we humans like predictability, comfort, reliability, and we form relationship attachments (to parents, husband, wife, children, lovers, and jobs) that are difficult to let go. We fear having things change.

Could it be that we don't trust God? Maybe we are not sure if God really knows what "HE" is doing? It seems that most of our fears in life go back to a primordial distrust in God. Maybe we need to help God out a little bit? So we reason, since we can't see God, and since God gave us free will and six senses, we had best use them. Have you ever caught yourself thinking this way? I have, and if you were honest with yourself, you would have to say that you have said or thought the same at some point in your life.

We must train ourselves in thought selection and thought control. If we do not, our thoughts will go through the stages of doubt →uncertainty →apprehension →anxiety →fear →gloom → doom →pessimism →depression. When this occurs our fear thought pattern becomes a rigidly fixed pattern and becomes a fixed behavior pattern, habit, or phobia. A phobia requires the services of a professional trained in the field of psychology to help you eradicate your problem, as it is often deep seated and may require several therapeutic counseling sessions using a process called systematic desensitization to help you progressively lessen or eradicate the rigidly structured behavioral pattern you have developed.

When we keep our thoughts focused on the past, we become depressed, bitter, and resentful. If we keep our thoughts focused on the future, speculating on every outcome, trying to out-guess God, we become apprehensive, anxiety-ridden, and fearful. When we let go and let God run the universe as "HE" chooses, we are able to decide in each moment how we will react to situations. When we do this, we begin to live in the "here and now." Then there is no fear because there is no second guessing or speculating about possible outcomes. Thus we have more energy and we feel more aliveness.

Fear is the unknown expectation about a situation, event, or person with a probability of consequence. It may be *real* or *imagined*. Fear makes us anxious, *block - ing our "inner light"* so it does not shine through. Which is true for you?

Fears That Handicap Us Most Are:
Fear of Expression, Low Self-Worth/Esteem
Fear of Being/Existing
Fear of Ill Health/Old Age
Fear of Non-Acceptance/Rejection (Criticism)
Fear of Loneliness/Isolation
Fear of Abandonment/Love
Fear of Appearing Stupid/Not Knowing
Fear of Change/Uncertainty
Fear of Failure/Success (Responsibility)
Fear of Poverty/Prosperity (Wealth)
Fear of Happiness/Enjoying Life

Fear is the unknown expectation about a situation, event, or person with the probability of consequences. Listed below are some common fears, check the ones that apply to you and rank each category from 1-5 or 1-6, 1 being

72

most fearful:

Professional

Fear of speaking in public

Failing an assignment

Fear of rejection

Loss of status

Fear of making decisions

Social

Fear of embarrassment

Fear a lack of conversational skills

Feelings of inferiority

Fear of being/acting dumb or stupid

Fear that you lack necessary social skills

Fear of being ignored

Personal

Fear of being alone

Lack of support

Feeling/expressing anger

Being too fat/thin

Growing old

Financial Fear

Being dependent

Being broke

Being poor

Being in debt

Lacking control/power

Lack of financial security

Financial losses/Financial future

Learn Ways You Can Handle Fear

Write out your answers below: Say to yourself, I respect my fears by acknowledging and admitting that I have them.

1. What faults or shortcomings do you admit to your and others, write them below.

2. Identify how your fears control you, stifle your
   emotional growth or creativity.
1.
2.
3.

Confront your fears; admit they are uncontrollable and
you are willing to work on their management. What is the
worst thing that could happen to you?

List action steps you will take today to manage your
fears:
1.
2.
3.

Everything that we say or do is programmed into our subconscious mind. To effectively manage stress, or fear we
will need to understand how the subconscious mind
works and gain mastery over it.

When we are fearful, angry, depressed, or anxious,
some common errors in thinking are: All or nothing
thinking. There are no gray or middle areas; you see
everything as black or white. On the other hand, you may
over generalize and see a single negative event as a
never-ending pattern of defeat. Or you may develop a
mental filter and pick out a single negative detail and
dwell on it until everything is affected by this particular
negative event.

Another thing you may do, is to disqualify the positive
event, or jump to conclusions by employing mind reading behavior. Here, you make a decision that someone is
responding negatively to you, without checking out the

facts; therefore your assumptions are in error. Other errors in thinking that occur when you are fearful, angry, or anxious are that you magnify or minimize a problem so that the events are thrown out of proportion to the facts.

Emotional reasoning can become a self-defeating behavior. You assume that the negative feelings you are experiencing are those of the real world, when in reality, the feeling state resides within your mind, body, and life experiences. It is a subjective experience that has been projected in your objective world as if it were a true state of being. To test if an event is real, list all of the objective data that can be quantified or verified through at least four of the senses (sight, hearing, touch, or sound) by a person who is neutral to the situation.

You lower your self-esteem by trying to improve yourself through the use of a should statement such as, "I should be able to handle this problem," or you mislabel your behavior when you fail to achieve what you desire, and call yourself stupid. This is negative self reinforcement. You are one with all the Intelligence in the universe, God.

AFFIRMATION

I am one with the Infinite. I am rocked in the Cradle of the Deep. To all outer details and distractions I am able to say, "It doesn't matter, just because it doesn't matter."

Chapter 5

LIGHT THE FIRE WITHIN YOU, MANAGE YOUR FEARS

Before we can fully focus on the needs of others, we need to be free of the fears that preoccupy our minds. Therefore we need to make progress in our own personal unfolding before we can serve humanity. The contribution you are able to make for the good of society is conditioned by the progress you make in your personal unfolding. When the lessons you need to learn are hard, you become preoccupied with your own pain and suffering. And you have little energy available to help others. It is difficult to focus on giving your gifts to others until you lighten the load of your burdens and inner turmoil.

Life is not easy. It was never intended to be easy. God never promised us a rose garden. To be human means we will experience human dilemmas and challenges. I believe that we were given a chance, prior to our entry to earth, to decide if we wanted to participate in this experience called life, and live as a spiritual being in a human body. I believe that we may have forgotten that we had this conversation with God. None of us was forced to be born into a body as a human being. We all chose and were allowed to come to earth to complete our upward climb to self mastery .We are here by divine appointment to do the Father's will. All of us agreed to achieve our soul perfection through helping to bring about God's kingdom on earth. After we arrived, it seems we lost the awareness that we were spiritual beings, having a human experience. So we began to behave from our lower nature

(Low Self), rather than our Divine nature (High Self). Due to our ignorance of our true nature, we allow ourselves to become beset with greed, fraud, malice, discontent, jealousy, envy, prejudice, hate, revenge, power, and control over the lives of others.

We were made in the image and likeness of God. We are here to help bring about God's kingdom on earth. God's kingdom, not our kingdom. I repeat this to myself every day, because I see so many of us playing God in the lives of others. Many of us have been called, but few are chosen for God's work on earth. You will only be chosen if you can listen to the small voice within as it speaks to you, telling you what to do, where you are to go, what you are to do, and with whom you are *supposed* to do God's bidding.

It is strange that we become fearful and disappointed. It seems as if we are expecting to walk around on a cloud all day. All of us came to earth to help and be of service to our fellow man. If you want to be an angel, to walk around and look all the time; you should not have asked to be born into a physical body that serves God and do "HIS" bidding.

I think we became fearful and disappointed, when we realized (some of us still have closed spiritual eyes) that we need to work out our soul's salvation. We do this by moving through our challenges, perplexities of human conflict, and personality conflicts.

None of us can remain babies forever. All babies are turned loose after nine months of gestation in the mother's uterus to grow and evolve into a human adult life. Then we begin our spiritual journey to attain Christ perfection. Remember, you are here for a reason.

Life is hard, and it is challenging. I have not discovered away, nor has anyone else, as to how we can avoid the perplexities, disappointments, and challenges of life. It is by divine illumination that you are reading this book right now. Accept that you are here to refine and express your divine self. All of us are here to get the polishing and fine tuning we need to live from our Christ presence.

You will be in a body until you have acquired the wisdom necessary to attain your Christhood. You can progress spiritually as far as you are willing to grow. Then you give up your physical body to experience the state called death. When you enter into this state, both you and God agree, you have learned all the lessons you are willing to learn. This does not mean that you have attained your state of Christ perfection. It only means you have stopped growing spiritually and desire release from your earth experience.

The state of death may be short or extended. God alone decides this. This is not for us to choose. God decides, based on our learning experience, how many revolutions we need before we are ready for eternal life. You can hasten this process if you are willing to move through the perplexities of the experience called life. To have mastery over your emotions and have no emotional investment in what is right or wrong. You shift into your divine self, where you do not take the things people say or do to you personally, because you realize they are acting from their state of Christ imperfection. So rather than get angry or annoyed with them, it wiser to go within to your Christ presence for clarity and divine illumination. Then say to yourself, from this exalted state of wisdom, "Father forgive them for they know not what they do; not my will, but thy will be done." Doing this will give you dominion and control over anything that anyone can say or do to you. Your objective is to be centered and focused so that you are not moved from your position of divine authority. You are of greatest service to God when you act as a vessel for God to flow through to help others.

Affirm and say to yourself, "I will give my best today.

I will live this day as if it were my last day on earth to do the good I came here to do." When you have learned and evolved to your Highest Self, you give up your human body to make your transition and depart in bliss.

In John 13:35, it says "By this shall all men know that ye are my disciples, if ye have love for one another. Love is the essence of all creation, so when you love you are expressing your godly nature. Truly love **is the only answer to any problem you will ever encounter**. Since God is Love and Love is God, God is the answer to all of your problems.

When you rise above your fears or the person who tugs at your emotional strings, you achieve self control and self mastery. Jesus says in Matthew 5:39, "But I say unto you, That ye resist not evil." He says to do good to those who would do you evil. It seems that our purpose is to love everyone and every thing. John 13:35 says, "By this shall all men know that ye are my disciples, if ye have love one to another." Love is the opposite of fear or misapprehension.

Our apprehensions, uncertainties, doubts, and fears keep us chained to earth and its experiences. The fear that paralyze most of us is the fear of expression. Most of us would rather die than stand before a group to speak.

A Fear of Self-Expression causes us to act timid and shy around others. Our low self-worth and sense of undeserving makes us feel unimportant. A distorted self-image can hold us back from speaking up to express ourselves. A fear of criticism and rejection underlies the fear of expression. We are ashamed to be the person we are because someone said we were not acceptable to them as we were. We were probably desperate for their acceptance at the time. However, did you ever check to see if this person likes himself? Anyone who is critical of another person will also be critical of himself, for we see and project from the inside out.

Whatever is inside us expresses outwardly, not inwardly. Too often we use others as a measure of who we are. God took great care to create no two persons alike. You are one of a kind, unlike any other person in the universe. Sometimes we are intimidated by others because we feel unworthy and undeserving. You did not create yourself, nor did your parents. They are the vessel God used to bring you forth onto the planet. Your parents were given permission to guide you, and keep you safe from harm until adulthood. Then they were to turn you over to God for your next phase of growth. Some parents play God and keep their children in bondage to them throughout life. Some children become dependent on their parents and see them as the source of their good. They are afraid to trust God as their source.

All parents need to tell their children to place their faith and trust in God alone, for God will be with them from birth to death. God is the one who will love and accept you in spite of your rejection of HIM. "Your lack of trust in Him, your lack of love, acceptance or dependence on Him to provide for your every need. God will never forsake or leave you alone. You will never be abandoned, humiliated, or rejected by God. God loves you with a fierce passion, unlike that of any person. You are his offspring, you are one with Him, for you are the expression of God; you were made in God I s image and likeness. You are wanted, loved, and needed by God.

You are a part of his plan to bring love, joy, peace, and harmony to the earth. You were especially chosen to be here. You have a right to all the love, abundance, prosperity, joy, peace, and happiness that is God. You are here by divine appointment. You are being allowed for the presence of God to express through you. You did not create yourself; therefore you can not destroy yourself. You do not belong to yourself. You belong to God. One day at a time, this is enough.

There are several emotional states that block our Divine inner light and prevent it from shining through us. They are: ***Enthusiasm, Joy, Bliss, and Love.***

What Is Your Experience With These Emotions?
Greed —
Jealousy —
Envy —
Revenge —
Anger —
Fear —

ONE DAY AT A TIME

Do not look back and grieve over the past, for it is gone; and do not be troubled about the future, for it has yet to come. Live in the present, and make it so beautiful that it will be worth remembering. IDA SCOTT TAYLOR

YOUR PART

Your good is here. Accept it!
Your joy is near! Embrace it!
Your Power is within. Harness it!
Your victory is now!
Claim it!
Your freedom is real. Declare it!
Your abundance is overflowing. Share it!
Your prosperity is good. Receive it!
Your problem is purposeful. Bless it!
Your spirit is divine. Free it!
Your love is great. Give it!
Your faith is mighty. Use it!
                    WILLIAM ARTHUR WARD

Fear of Happiness or Enjoying Life is a belief that you are unworthy to exist on the planet, and will cause you to question whether you deserve to be alive. It is wise to not

81

think too highly or too lowly of yourself. Remember, we live and breathe through the body of Christ. You are now living in the body you possess by the divine appointment and plan of God and God gives you the free will to decide how you will live out your life. The key word here is to live life to its fullest until your departure from the planet. For God is the only one who knows exactly when we will depart this life, and this He does not reveal to anyone.

To get information and answers about your mission in life, you need to go within to listen to the voice of God. When we are able to become still and listen to the voice of God within us, we receive the answers we need.

Divine information from God is only revealed to us when we are peaceful and quiet within. Then we can experience that inner state of quiet where we are free of anger, strife, malaise, revenge, jealously, animosity, conflict, anxiety, fear. All of the emotions just mentioned robs us of vitality For they allow us to become one with the negative roller coaster sensations of our life. We become fearful of having a life of joy and happiness, so we become preoccupied with the gloom and doom situations surrounding us. If allowed to continue, this soon becomes a norm in our life as we continue to create and recreate our negative and destructive life dramas.

When we learn effective ways to cope with our problems, we create a new life pattern that allows us to evolve spiritually. If we are unable to find effective coping skills, we become preoccupied with the doom and gloom events which create a down and depression within us. Then we fail to see the good in anything or anyone, especially ourselves. At these times, it seems that everyone is okay. except us. And we feel this way because our attention is focused on what a horrible person we are (or terrible sinner if you are a Christian). It is true; we all fall short of the kingdom and glory of God. However, we are not worms of the dust. There are times when we may behave in a lowly manner, but we are not worms. We were created in the image and likeness of God and that is exciting.

Fear of Being Who You Are is the result of low self-esteem. When we esteem someone we behold the good in them for we know they count and make a difference in the total scheme of life. We can usually see this for others, but we fail to see our own positive attributes. It is good to have humility and to not be egotistical, but we do not need to go to the opposite extreme and belittle ourselves without mercy. Life is about balance. We should not think more highly of ourselves than we deserve but we must never feel that we are the worst of all humankind. Truly, the rain shines on the just and unjust alike.

Our fears are the barriers that hold us back and keep us locked into nonproductive behaviors, activities; and relationships. When we experience thoughts of fear, everything in our world appears to be out of focus. The mental images we send out may be clear but our mind distorts the image inside of us based on our inner picture of our self image.

We are electrically charged energy systems. On a physical plane, this manifests as our drive or enthusiasm (God in us) and creates within us a fire (energy, light) that propels us toward our desires, dream and goals. *As we move through our fears, we light the fire within us.* "If the Son makes you free, you will be free indeed." — John 8:36 We must develop a character trait unlike fear to help us focus on the divinity within us and all people.

A patient person is filled with an awareness of God, so there is no place in their life for hurry, worry, or anxiety. When we are poised and centered in our Christ mind, nothing can disturb our calm, serene nature. The characteristics of a patient person are expansion, perception, kindness, and consideration. A patient person does not mind waiting because waiting gives them time to commune with the divine presence within. All things will come to those who have the patience to wait for them.

Patience dissolves the illusion of time and its false measurement of fast and slow. To be a patient person is likened to being immersed in the essence of the Christ. Learning to be patient with yourself and others provides you with an opportunity to express your full potential because it teaches you how to center yourself into a state of inner tranquility and peace. You learn how to enjoy the blessed quietness that surrounds you for you are being immersed in the timelessness and spacelessness of the universe. Decide today to live in the here and now.

This is where you need to be. For there is nowhere else to go. Take time to give your full attention to this moment of your life for this is the only moment of eternity you will know about. Be glad to be alive. Do not be in a hurry for life to pass. Be patient with your feelings. Be gentle with yourself and others. Take time to observe yourself to learn from your mistakes. Listen to the "voice within" as it teaches you about yourself, about others, and about life.

LET NOT YOUR HEART BE TROUBLED

Let not your heart be troubled;
*   you need not be afraid.*
You need not fear the outcome
*   before your prayers are prayed.*
Tomorrow's still a mystery,
*   and yesterday is gone. ..*
Thank God for everything today,
*   and know you're not alone.*
Our Lord has promised comfort
*   in seasons of distress,*
And He will not forsake those

who seek His holiness.
You need not fear the darkness
for God has promised light,
So let not your heart be
troubled throughout the darkest night.
CLAY HARRISON

Chapter 6

THE CAUSES OF FEAR

I claim that in back of all fear is a distrust of God. We are afraid to trust someone that we cannot see with our own eyes and feel with our hands to take care of and provide for us. In Luke 12:27-33, Jesus tells us "Look at the lilies. They don't toil and spin, and yet Solomon in all his glory was not robed as well as they are. And if God provides clothing for the flowers that are here today and gone tomorrow, don't you suppose that He will provide clothing for you, you doubters? And don't worry about food, what to eat and drink; don't worry at all that God will provide it for you." "All mankind scratches for its daily bread, but your heavenly Father know your needs. He will always give you all you need from day to day if you will make the kingdom of God your primary concern. So don't be afraid, little flock. For it gives your Father great happiness to give you the kingdom." Again, in Mark 11:22-25, "If you only have faith in God — this is the absolute truth — you can say to this Mount of Olives, "Rise up and fall into the Mediterranean, and your command will be obeyed. All that's required is that you really believe and have not doubt. Listen to me. You can pray for anything and if you believe, you have it; it's yours."

The primary cause of all fears has to do with our relationship to God. I am not talking about the natural fear of flight reaction to protect our safety. We have been taught and have learned to fear God. However, we need to be in "awe of," "reverent," "bow in submission in our heart to God's holy name." We do not need to fear God.

It makes you wonder if we are not still working through our fear expectations of God's punishment when we disobeyed God in the Garden of Eden.

There are many secondary reasons for our pervasive fear syndrome. One of them is to have a "Be Perfect Script" (Transactional Analysis). A "Be Perfect Script" says, "1 can't make mistakes, I can't be vulnerable, I can't let others know that I don't know or have all of the answers. I once thought that if I didn't have the answers or know all the answers, it showed me as being stupid. Also, I was afraid that I might impose on someone if I asked them to explain something to me that I did not understand. Illogical and irrational thinking indeed.

Much of our illogical and irrational thinking is based on superstition, our acceptance of folklore, and faulty reasoning embraced by a parent, grand parent, or significant others years prior to our birth. All the beliefs, ideas, and opinions of our ancestors reside inside us and are acted out daily in our lives as here and now experiences. Young children often misinterpret or misquote the things they hear and see as they imitate the adults in their life.

If you have an unfounded fear and there is no objective data to support your behavior, you may be acting out the beliefs of another or the behavior of a prior time in your life history or that of a relative who has made their transition from the planet.

Another cause of fear is the reliance on one's own effort. As I stated earlier, I learned to distrust at an early age, so I became independent at a young age; I felt that I could not trust anyone to take care of or assist me.

Self sufficiency is a little different from relying on one's own efforts. When I am self-sufficient, I feel no one is as smart as me. When someone takes this attitude, they place a great burden on themselves because they are saying to the other person, "you are not as smart as me and

I can only depend on my judgment; I don't trust your judgment. In actuality, it is their judgment they mistrust, but they don't realize it. This person may come across as acting superior to others when, under the surface, they suffer from an inferiority complex. There is always a dual side to every personality character.

If we have feelings of superiority, we will also have feelings of inferiority, and either side of the emotional coin can appear at any given moment. If we are afraid to show feelings of inferiority because it projects an image of stupidity, then we may show the flip side of this behavior and act as if we were superior to others and that we know, or have, all of the answers.

Every character trait has both its positive and negative components. The opposing component of fear is confidence. There is a dual nature to all personality traits. Therefore, we may feel and display both fear or confidence at airy given time before the behavioral habit strength is learned on a cellular level in the brain.

Still another secondary cause of fear is our need for independence. Independence may be expressed as a fear of attachment or closeness in a relationship. A person might either be afraid to form a committed relationship or, if they are in a relationship, they may fear that the other person might leave them, so they behave in a clinging fashion to their significant other, to mask their true feelings of independence.

A fear of freedom may express itself as a limitation physically, mentally or spiritually. Spiritually this would manifest as a sense of lack and limitations. What we lack is trust in God, or in God I s ability to provide for our daily needs. Here, our sense of reliance on our own ability (freedom) interferes with our need to form a close relationship (fear of commitment) of bonding to either a human or spiritual personality. It seems that the spiritual bonding is the most challenging for us, because we are taught in our society to trust and believe only in what we see, feel, touch, or hear through our physical senses.

In the physical world a sense of lack and limitation may be seen as a poverty consciousness. Hence someone may seem financially strapped for their daily needs all the time. The fear of letting go, or trusting in a presence we can not see is awesome and frightening to those of us who are taught educationally to trust only in our physical senses of what we see, feel, touch or hear .

Ultimately we lose our freedom to evolve spiritually because we are enslaved in a physical world of sensation. We lack the insight or courage to let go of our old self-image and habits, to discover new horizons of being, feeling, or doing.

We are creatures of habit, and we only let go of old ways of doing and being when it creates tremendous emotional pain. Most of us would rather hang on to what is uncomfortable and does not work than to try something new that we think *might* work.

Our fear of change allows us to remain in unworkable, painful, and self destructive relationships. When we do this, we stifle both our emotional and spiritual growth. It is also possible to be very wealthy and have an unful-filled sense of lack and limitation, a "not enough " syndrome. This creates a sense of emptiness and deprivation that can only be alleviated through a deep trusting and emotional relationship with your higher power, which I choose to call God. This higher power that I call God is called many things in other religions. It may be referred to as Allah, Christ, First Cause, Lord, Life, Universal Principle, The Way, Tao, and by many other titles that I may fail to mention.

It has become apparent to me, as I speak to people of different faiths, nationalities, and philosophical persuasions that we are all talking about the same power, energy, or force. We are just looking at this from a different angle, and it is all right with me to allow this difference so that I might feel a sense of sister, and brotherhood, oneness, closeness, with all people.

Chapter 7

FAITH GIVES THE EXTRA MILEAGE

Both fear and faith are identical, in that the energy used in the one is the same energy as that used in the other. Both are a thought and they are identical in their mental action. Fear is a *positive acceptance you will experience that which you dislike*. And faith is a *positive acceptance you will experience that which you like*. The energy of fear converted into faith will produce an effect the exact opposite. Faith is the expectation of the unexpected. It is an open heart. It is surrender to life's sovereign will, in submission to the ruling order of the universe, to a mental acceptance of and belief in good.

Faith is the power to see in the disappointment of today the fulfillment of tomorrow, in the end of old hopes the beginning of new life. Faith is the inward power to see beyond the outward signs, the power to know that all is right when everything appears wrong. When your fondest dreams go amiss and your prayers seem to remain unanswered, faith is the vision of life that soars beyond the limitations of the small self. Faith—these narrow senses, this imperfect reason, this drift of circumstances—sees that our life is a part of something more than we have understood, that in spite of all that seems, and all that may happen, there is an ultimate fulfillment that all is well. That all must be well; for life has an eternal meaning. You are one with the infinite. Whatever befalls you in the enfolding, unfolding process of life will work out for your good.

To have such faith is to have the serenity of the saint, the passion of the poet, and the exaltation of the mystic.

Faith is an attitude toward life, a feeling about life. It comes out of inward growth. If you cannot believe in much, then believe in the little that you can. Start where you are and grow. What seed can have foreknowledge of the tree it will become? Faith grows from continuous questioning of our motive and motivation about our daily activities.

If you find yourself deploring how little your faith is, think how far you have come with the little faith you have. The faith that grows out of questioning is stronger than the faith born of blind acceptance. The entrapment paradigm of dependency must be avoided with its concomitant feelings of anxiety, doom, and gloom. This state of mind does not foster a feeling of trust; so you have no foundation to build on for faith. If you cannot trust yourself and others, it will be difficult to establish a sense of certainty and faith in God. Self-doubt is personally and spiritually damaging. Both doubt and faith have the same energy vibration. They require the same amount of energy expenditure. The difference is attitude. The same is true for success and failure.

All activity in life begins as thought, then proceeds to action, then manifestation. Fear is the result of a block in your energy. A given behavior is not acted out for many reasons: unfamiliar terrain, expectation of adverse consequences, uncertainty of outcome, avoidance of risk, and avoidance of uncomfortable situations.

Anytime we place ourselves in the center of the universe and focus on the lower case "i" (God at the human level) rather than the upper case "I" God (universal); we experience fear. The lower case "I," fears the effect of too much power. It is afraid of being overpowered by another ego.

The person who places things in their right perspective knows that the power of mankind is shared with the Divine Mind of God, and that God works through mankind to bring about HIS kingdom on earth. We are the hand, feet, and eyes of God. ***God can only do for us what he can do through us*** (the human race of mankind) .When we get an accurate perception of this and know that we know, there will no longer be anything to fear.

God never leaves us alone to figure things out on our own. Divine help is always available. We need to be able to humble ourselves, to let go of self pride and ego. Then we can ask for help by saying, "not my will Lord, but let thy will be done in my body, my life and in my affairs." This takes trust in a God we can not see through human eyes, but we trust, through our faith in God's word that He would never leave us alone. Faith is another word for trust. When we decide not to trust God and to exercise our free will, we are afraid to make any decision. Oftentimes the decisions we make are clouded by our human judgment and shortcomings. And the results are doubt and indecision.

Because of our fear, we wonder if we have made the right decision. Doubtful thoughts will never enter into our minds when we accept the fact that we are co-creators with the divine mind of God, and that we can never make a mistake. As we allow God to work through our body, mind, and affairs, our life is transformed. It then becomes the handiwork and masterpiece of the Lord. We become a strange creature to others because we are ruled by God's holy ordinance.

We are in the world, but not of the world. Others may not understand our actions and reactions, but we know that things of the spirit are not always comprehended through the physical sensual world. We were given a physical body so that our "soul" could evolve, become refined by working through our emotions of fear and anger. Our goal is not to eliminate fear and anger, but to use them in a just and right way.

When we come into the light of truth and acknowledge ourselves as one with the divine mind of God, we are guided as to the right use of anger and fear. There is such a thing as righteous indignation which Jesus used in the temple. No one was harmed by Jesus' display of anger. Jesus was guided as to the right use of anger through the divinity within Him.

It may be hard to accept that you are divine. And maybe even harder to think that you have the same powers as Jesus. Jesus said, "If you have faith as a grain of mustard seed, you can say to this mountain, move hence and yonder, and it shall be done unto you." I have struggled with this thought for years, because I was trying to get the faith and fixation of purpose like Jesus, and I felt unequal to the task. However, Jesus said, "Greater things than I do will you do." I was confused and did not want to elevate myself to the level of Jesus. I felt Jesus was greater than I, so I figured God would send the person, or speak to the heart of the person He wanted to do His will.

I now realize that Jesus is seeking both you and me, to daily, die to our old nature, to pick up our cross and follow in His footsteps. We do not have the faith as Jesus because we have not taken time to develop the self discipline needed to surrender our will to the divine will of God and say, "not my will but thy will be done in my mind, body, and affairs." We have to be in the world, but not of it.

There are a lot of exciting things in the world that pull at our heartstring. It is a miracle when we can have or show any faith in God's ability to handle our affairs. The truth of the matter is that Jesus was <u>greater than both you and me in His use of faith.</u> It is true that Jesus was God's son. But so are we God's children. We are direct descendants of Adam and Eve, the first humans God created. We did not make ourselves. "So God created Man in his own image, in the image of God he created them; male and female."

Jesus was in tune with the divine mind of God within Him. He knew the will of God for his earthly journey, and was willing to be guided on the path God would have Him follow. Jesus was chosen to come to earth for a special mission and that was to show mankind, you and I, what was the will of God for our spiritual evolvement, so we could rise above the everyday nuances of human existence. If we could use an inkling of the faith that Jesus used, we could move through our everyday challenges without trepidation or fear, full of praise and thankfulness that we have within us a power that overcomes all obstacles when we are in touch with it.

The divine spirit of the Lord moves through us. It has been implanted in our hearts. However, if our heart is filled with malice, anger, fear, envy, greed, and ill will toward our fellow man, the spirit of the Lord will depart from us. As our faith and trust in God grows stronger, we realize that of our own, we are powerless to change ourselves or our lives. By our faith, and trust in the God to guide and protect us, we are conquerors. Through our belief and faith in God, we can move through any obstacle or challenge victoriously without doubt or fear of the outcome.

Faith is the key. Faith is an expectancy of good. Fear is an expectancy of gloom and doom, the worst outcome. We see, live, and experience the world from the inside to the outside. We create pictures in our mind through the words we think and the pictures inside our mind. And just like on a movie screen, the images within reflect outside us through our words, deeds, and actions. We create in the moment. When we are fearful, we distort the truth and circumstances and may succumb to debased behavior, because our trust in a power outside us. When we place our trust in the physical world of effects, anything can and often does happen. Our experiences can be unsettling and frightening.

We receive and experience the world according to the beliefs we hold inside us, our expectations. Therefore, we always receive what we expect. If you have learned to expect the worst, each time a new situation arises you will experience what you expect-for better or worst. As we grow in our faith, we learn to expect a good outcome because we realize that God wants us to have the best and be the best.

When your inner pictures become positive, your inner and outer experiences change for the better. As we increase our positive expectancy level, we create more associational pairings of thought in our brain, our behavior, and in our outer world of experience. We no longer fear the worst.

When we learn to fear the worst, it automatically happens. Because you have learned to condition your mind and body to respond to a given thought pattern. It is difficult to analyze, or cure, a thought pattern. Thought patterns are very fleeting and insidious. What we may call idling of thoughts (daydreaming), can be a reinforcement of a destructive thought pattern. Negative and destructive thoughts are worse for you than to be robbed at gunpoint. When you are robbed; you see and feel something happening through your senses physiologically, and you respond to it. When we are confronted with a negative thought, either our own or that of another person, we put up no defenses and allow the negative thought to enter. A robber can be apprehended and put in jail. It is not so with a negative thought. Learn to become more aware of negative thought patterns every day, and cancel them out of your mind. Repeat the word cancel, cancel until you no longer feel the negative thought or feeling.

We must be conscious every moment of our life of whom and what we are; why we exist on this planet, and how we can make our life more fulfilling and enriching. Distrust and doubt cause fear. Distrust is a fear of the unknown and a desire for a certainty of outcome that causes most of our anxiety. We are so accustomed to being able to predict a possible outcome that we become entrapped in our own personal creations of habit formation.

We must replace distrust with trust and doubt with assurance. Trust is the building block for our eventual foundation of faith. The key here is to develop a faith in God's goodness that is unshakable. **Affirm and say to yourself:**

I am free from all fear. I have a strong and vital faith. My faith makes me whole.

There is nothing I cannot do, cannot be, when I decide on a goal in life and stay on target.

I now bow down and worship with childlike innocence, the perfect life God has given me. I am never alone.

"Yea, though I walk through the valley of the shadow of death, I will fear no evil; for thou art with me; thy rod and thy staff they comfort me."

The Lord is my shepherd, I trust HIM to guide and protect me.

I have faith in God's justice; therefore, I do not fear any person, place, or thing.

I put on my spiritual armor and go forth into life with renewed strength, vigor, and determination to be free from the emotion of fear.

Focus on being more alive each day, each hour, and each minute. If you do this, you will soon be able to say: *.fear* **stopped by our house to visit, everyone was busy partic - ipating in the activity of the moment; fear had no one to talk to, or entertain it, so it passed on to visit another dwelling.**

Write what you have learned about faith below:

Chapter 8

WHAT IS THE FIRE WITHIN YOU?

Your Fire within is the living presence of God, Divine Spirit, Higher Power, Holy Spirit. This life force came into your body with your first breath and it departs from your body with your last breath. There are many factors that can blot out your inner fire or light. They are fear and trust. Both are connected to the birthing process. At the time of birth, we decide if our environment is safe, and if our needs will be met. We learn to trust or not to trust. Trust gives us a feeling of security and safety. Then we are free to explore outside relationships other than our parents.

Who can you trust? We can trust those persons who do not hurt us, sexually abuse us or exploit our feelings. When this happens we have conquered the Trust factor. If we do not, we develop **fear**, rather than **trust**. Fear is the most powerful of all emotions. It blocks our life force energy, allowing us to act timid, and unsure of ourselves. Then we develop an underlying fear, that pervades every aspect of ourselves, and we become afraid of the unknown.

Why are we afraid of the unknown? We are we afraid of the unknown because we do not know whom to trust. We experience uncertainty in our life rather than certainty. We do not have predictability, or sameness. This sameness is having a constant love source, or nurturer, to attend to our basic needs for safety and survival. Our fire, or life force needs tender loving care to keep it shining brightly. We all have a fire, but for many of us, it is barely lit. ***The situations and events that "wipes out" our*** *fire within are: **Doubt, Disappointment, Despair, Sadness, Hurt, Loneliness, Lack of or Loss of love, Rejection, Constant Criticism, Isolation, and feelings of Abandonment.*** Affirmations are a helpful tool to create new ways of thinking to produce new feelings.

Affirmations
Stay in the present. Avoid statements like, "I will" or "I hope to." Instead, say, "I am."

Work on only a few affirmations at a time. To help you get started, I have made a list of affirmations. After you get used to them, you may want to substitute others that more closely apply to your individual situation. Remember each time to fill in your own name after the "I". Here are some suggested affirmations that you can begin working with to increase your personal sense of empowerment.

Fears of the Unknown *Insert your name below*
1. I. . . . . am experiencing new things (job, relationship) even though they are scary or unfamiliar.

2. I. . . . . have the courage to speak, my true feelings, lovingly to others.

3 I . . . . am willing to face the unknown even though it is scary.

4. I . . . . want to be satisfied in my life so I am willing to take risks.

5. I. . . . . am taking the risks to get what I want, even though I am scared.

6. I. . . . . have the courage to do what it takes to get what I want and need.

7. I . . . . want to say when I retire that I did what I wanted to do.

8. I . . . . want to be able to say on my dying bed that I faced all my fears.

9. I . . . . am visualizing the way I want my job and/or relationship to be.

How to Light Your Fire Within

Energy → **Enthusiasm** → **Fire** → **Aliveness** → **Light** → **Fire = Goal/vision** → **Focus** → **Enthusiasm** → **Fire**

Fears blot out energy, enthusiasm, fire, aliveness/light. It is only when you are fearful, have feelings of superiority, that you feel unrelated to the people around you, isolated, and a stranger. Spiritually we are all related. Our true parents are our heavenly Father/Mother, not our earthly parents.

An appreciation of esthetics allows you to connect with the nonhuman world of nature. The ocean, waterfall, star, sun, moon, sky, a tree, painting, statue, dramatic play, music, musical instrument, a song, a bird, and an airplane are all works of beauty. God our Higher Power, Supreme Being, helps us see a larger view of the world, our place in it, and our connection to it. All has value and is valuable. The following Vision of Enoch summarizes this.

GOD SPEAKS TO MANKIND
I speak to you.
Be still, know that I am God.
I spoke to you when you were born
Be still, know that I am God.
I spoke to you at your first sight.
Be still, know that I am God.

I spoke to you At your first word.
Be still, know that I am God.

I spoke to you At your first thought.
 Be still, know that I am God.
I speak to you Through the dew of the morning.
Be still, know that I am God.
I speak to you Through the peace of the evening.
Be still, know that I am God.

 I speak to you Through the storm and the clouds
Be still, know that I am God.
I speak to you Through the grass of the meadows.
Be still, know that I am God.

I speak to you Through the trees of the forest.
Be still, know that I am God.
I speak to you Through the valleys and the hills.
Be still, know that I am God.

I speak to you Through the Holy Mountains.
Be still, know that I am God.
I speak to you Through the rain and the snow.
Be still, know that I am God.

I speak to you Through the waves of the sea.
Be still, know that I am God.
I speak to you Through the splendor of the sun.
Be still, know that I am God.

I speak to you Through the brilliant stars.
Be still, know that I am God.

I speak to you When you are alone.
Be still, know that I am God.
THE ESSENE GOSPEL OF PEACE — BOOK TWO

Our Fire Within Manifests In Many Ways

Your fire within manifests as Desire, Goal Achievement, Vitality, Enthusiasm, Aliveness, Joy, Love, Happiness, Light, Fire. In light there are the emotions-love compassion, and understanding. In darkness, there is anger, fear, and hate. If we focus on our inner darkness, we will be consumed by it. Whereas, when we dwell in the light of the universe, God, we are connected to our inner Christ nature. The universal light of God connects us to our inner source, and helps us to express our true being. Anger, worry, doubt, and fear disconnect us from this source and prevent us from knowing our real selves (emotional, social, physical, spiritual). Where is your fire? You can't give something that you do not have.

When you are enlightened, you experience your unlimited potential. And when you are in darkness, you act as limited beings. When we are filled with the Christ Light, we are full of universal love, not human secular love. The universal love of the Christ Mind is able to overcome lack, limitation, envy, greed, jealousy, anger, misunderstanding, sadness, loneliness, disappointment, rejection, work slow down, work stoppage, unemployment, unfairness, injustice, conflict, antagonism, and fear

When we are fearful, we lack courage. Courage allows us to persist in the right direction in the face of fear, trusting divine intuition to guide us. Because we are filled with light and fire, the doors of the universe obey our every command. Do you have light? Do you have any fire? Where is it? Where is your fire? You cannot give away something you do not have. No matter how much you desire others to have fire, or how important it seems for others to get or have fire; you must tend your own fire first. For when the fire is out for you, it is out for everyone associated with you. You must overcome the darkness of your own mind and of others. We do this through heart to heart communication.

Your ability to communicate with others depends a lot on your ability to connect with them on a heart to heart level. When you communicate to motivate yourself or others, the words you use and the way you use them are critical. When you communicate using Soft Power Negotiation Skills™ and Soft Power Words™ people hear what you say. Therefore, you are able to motivate them. When we are motivated, we are excited, energetic, enthusiastic, have drive, stamina, and we are alive with light and fire.

When we are unmotivated we are lifeless, rather than alive. Our excitement, energy, drive, joy, peace, stamina, love, and enthusiasm are the source of an inner state of aliveness I refer to as "The Fire Within You." Some people refer to this as charisma. However, it is more than mere charisma. It makes an ordinary person extraordinary. When we are on fire with energy, drive, and enthusiasm we glow. We are alive with an inner joy, peace, and contentment that no human can give. Our light within shines outside of us as a sense of contentment, peace, love, joy, bliss, motivation, and aliveness. It causes us to have good feelings about ourselves. It is the way we see ourselves in relation to others. In Matthew 5:14-16, Jesus says "Ye are the light of the world. A city that is set on an hill cannot be hid. Neither do you light a candle, and put it under a bushel, but on a candlestick; and it gives light unto all that are in the house. Let your light so shine before others that, they see your good works, and glorify your Father in Heaven." It is your job to keep your fire lit, no matter the disappointments, setbacks, or hardships. Acknowledge the problems, but don't buy into the gloom and doom. It will affect your motivation and energy level. This is where "fake it until you make it" comes in.

Mastery in the following areas can help sustain your energy, and drive to maintain your inner fire/light: 1. Personal leadership development 2. Open communication 3. Manage fears that block your *Highest Self.* 4. Move through personal barriers (anger, resentment, envy). It says in Matthew 5:22-25, "Whosoever is angry with his brother without a just cause shall be in danger of the judgment; and who shall say, thou fool, shall be in danger of hell fire. Therefore if thou bring thy gift to the altar, and there remember that thy brother hath ought against thee; Leave thy gift before the altar, and go thy way; first be reconciled to thy brother, and then come offer thy gift. Agree with thy adversary quickly, whilst thou art in the way with him." All of this is meant to say that your greatest enemy is within you. You must remember to let no one, including yourself, steal your joy. Both your inner joy and light have been placed inside you by God, to be an inspiration to others.

Remember to keep your light lit. Remove yourself from anyone or anything that would keep you from behaving or being your Best Self, your "Christ Self." Matthew 5:22 says, "If thy right eye offend thee, pluck it out, and cast it from thee: for it is profitable for thee that one of thy member should perish, and not that thy whole body." "Let your communication be Yea, or Nay, for whatsoever is more than these come of evil, "Matthew 5:43. Honor your commitments. keep your word, do what you say you will do. This helps you develop self discipline. When you have self discipline, you are less likely to be fearful. And when you keep fear at a minimum, your fire is lit, your glow shines brightly, as others see your Christ light.

What is the fire within you? It is: freedom from conflict-antagonism, freedom from prejudice-prejudging. It is the sparkle in your eyes, the contagion of your smile, it is forgiveness, kindness, your dream or desire, desire to excel, desire to become better, enthusiasm, compassion, light, love, joy, and self mastery. You are responsible to light your fire and to keep it lit. Acknowledge that you cannot control others, the world, or yourself. To have control over your thoughts, your tongue, and your emotions is self mastery.

Your fire within is peaceful thoughts and feelings, it is awareness of the "all" of life, it is your connection to every human being on the planet. It is at "Onement" with God. You will have more fire as you get your self out the way, surrender to God, and allow this force to move through your body and life to do its divine will. To the degree that you surrender yourself, will be the magnitude of your fire within. Write what you have learned from this section.

What Is Happiness
Everything outside of us is an illusion for which we sacrifice our life force and mind to obtain, while we ignore the light within us. Reverend Gabriel Cousens, has this to say about happiness. "For to weigh thy happiness, according to that which may befall thee, is to live as a slave. And to live according to the angels, which speak within thee, is to be free. In this doth happiness lie: To know what is your sunshine and what is not. The Bible says "if thou dost desire and seek after that which doth not belong to thee, then shall thou surely lose that which is Thine."

If you would have eternal life, hold fast to the eternity within you, and grasp not at the shadows of the world of men and women, which hold the seed of death. Do not barter that which is eternal for that which can die in an hour."

IT IS TIME:

To devote yourself to God completely;
To keep God before your mind continuously;
To give IT your love unconditionally;
To allow ITS Light and Love to fill you;

To share all your wonderful gifts with others;
To pray for yourself and others unceasingly.
It is Time; It is Time.

ESSENE NEWSLETTER, OCTOBER 1995

Chapter 9

HOW TO LIGHT THE FIRE WITH YOU

The questions you need to continually ask yourself are, "How do I feel about myself?" Do I like the person I am becoming *or* have become? How can I refine my behavior, and learn more about myself to become a better person? To be healed spiritually you need to work on the relationship between your inner self (man and woman) to bring about a rebirth of your inner child. When the child within you is reborn, you become a new person. You are no longer your old self. So you behave differently. We need to learn how to respect and appreciate each other and move from a competitive mind set to more cooperation. We need to learn to express our individual creativity, our intuitive genius, and freedom through peaceful means. We need to move from friction to harmony. Our goal is to live a life without friction (conflict).

We often feel a need to overcome something to enjoy life. Our need to cope with life is the result of an erroneous assumption that we have personal power, and that we can get what we want through friction and conflict. We do not have power. We use the energy of the universal presence, power, intelligence, and vitality of God, that continually express through out the universe. God expresses through us as Infinite Good, Infinite Intelligence, and Divine Consciousness. We use the mind of God in all the Good things that we do. Likewise, we use our lower nature in worry, doubt, greed, malice, jealousy, envy, revenge, corruption, hate, conflict, and evil intention. A higher power, force/energy, and intelligence are in control of the universe. We can tap into this force and use this energy to create any good thing we desire as long as it serves the needs of others as well as ourselves. Whenever we use this Divine force! energy for evil purposes or intent, it brings destruction upon us. God the Good is Omnipresence, Omnipresent, Creative, Peace, Abundance, Intelligence, Contentment, Prosperity, Joy, and Love. We need to seek a life of harmonious living without friction, conflict, pain, or disagreements. This is why Jesus said, "If your right hand offends you cut it off," (if your hands cause you to steal, it is better to be without hands, so you do not sin by stealing. Likewise, if your tongue causes you to lie, gossip, or speak evil about your neighbor, it is better to be without a tongue so you do not sin. A sin is any error, mistake, where you miss the mark and behave from your lower nature rather than your Christ Nature. God has implanted his spirit within us, but we have to activate it, invite it into our life by deciding to live a just and pure life. The choice is ours.

We can experience worry, doubt, fear, disharmony, anguish, pain, misery, anxiety, discontent, poverty, sickness, disease, and mental turmoil. Or we can travel the High Road by behaving in a just manner, being, kind, considerate, understanding, compassionate, truthful, honest, and be in control of our negative emotions (anger, rebellion, defiance, hostility, hate, prejudging others, hot temper). Likewise we can have integrity, patience, be quiet within to have peace and stillness.

There are a number of techniques we can use to develop our impure nature. We can calm our discordant energies and emotions through focused breathing, calm music, deep therapeutic body work, acupuncture, yoga, exercise, dance, or creative works (ballet, painting, drama, sculpting, and writing).

We can ascend to our Higher Nature, the Christ Self, through prayer, meditation, and quiet contemplation upon the nature of God or Jesus, with the intention to walk and live from this consciousness twenty-four hours a day. This is a worthy goal to seek. Whether you attain perfection or not, if you start on the path to become the Christ, your Higher/Best self you will come closer to your goal by trying, than if you stay where you are and tell yourself you can never be God, Jesus, or Buddha. No one will ever be Jesus. But we can behave like Jesus, or any enlightened deity we respect. And we can strive to live by the principles they taught. Jesus talked about kindness, gentleness of spirit, compassion, understanding, peace, harmony, joy, purity of thought, forgiveness seventy, times seventy, repentance, obedience, cooperation, meekness (humility), contentment, love, a faith that is unshakable in the face of disappointment or hardship. You need to know God will take of you, if you *trust, believe, and have faith.* Jesus said "It is done unto you as you believe." When we live from this exalted state of mind, gloom, doom, depression, disappointment, discouragement, sadness, loneliness, lack, limitation, or poverty mind set cannot attach itself to us.

When you travel the High Road of consciousness, you are hopeful, peaceful, enthusiastic, excited, joyous, contented, and feel at one with the spirit of God. In this state nothing can disturb the calm peace of your soul. Jesus said "In the world ye shall have tribulations, but be of good cheer, I have overcome the world (meaning I have been where you are, I overcame that, I paid the price for you by being the sacrificial lamb, so your mind can be at peace). God is our Royal High Priest and Priestess. If you do not believe in God, just try to keep yourself alive, forever, through your human will.

I am glad God has a way to humble all of us who are arrogant, pious, and feel that we created the earth and own it. We came into this earth with nothing and we leave out with nothing. Ashes to ashes, and dust to dust we become.

There are natural ways to have more energy so that you feel more alive and on fire with enthusiasm and joy. The foods we eat make a difference in the way we feel. We are what we eat. If we eat foods that generate life giving energy, we will be energized. If we eat foods that are lifeless, we will feel lifeless.

The foods we eat can bring energy and life to the cells of our body or they can take away energy and life from the cells of our body, according to Leonard Taylor, who has researched this field. He has identified the 51 healthiest foods for a vegetarian and the 53 healthiest non vegetarian foods. You can write him to get a list of these foods and others for a nominal fee. Leonard's address is listed in the bibliography.

53 Healthiest Non-Vegetarian

Apple – Plum – Banana
Asparagus – Avocado – Cranberries
Barley – Beans – Bell Pepper
Broccoli – Cauliflower – Brussels Sprouts
Dates – Grapefruit – Grapes
Eggplant – Garlic – Corn
Collard Greens – Mustard – Cabbage
Carrot – Celery – Chili Pepper
Cinnamon – Clove – Ginger
Fish – Turkey
Kale – Tomato – Mushroom
Nuts – Oats
Olive Oil – Onion – Tea
Parsley – Prunes
Potato – Sweet Potato – Pumpkin
Rice – Soybean – Spinach
Strawberries – Raspberries – Blueberries
Melon – Watermelon – Orange
Wheat bran (cereal) – Yogurt

51 Healthiest Vegetarian Foods

That Can help light the fire of aliveness within the cells of your body are:

Apple – Asparagus – Avocado
Banana – Barley – Beans
Bell Pepper – Blueberries
Broccoli – Cauliflower
Collard Greens – Mustard – Cabbage
Carrot – Celery – Chili Pepper
Cinnamon – Clove
Brussels Sprouts – Corn – Cranberries
Dates – Eggplant – Garlic
Ginger – Grapefruit – Grapes
Kale – Tomato – Mushroom
Nuts – Oats
Olive Oil – Onion – Tea
Parsley – Plums – Prunes
Potato – Sweet Potato – Pumpkin
Rice – Soybean – Spinach
Strawberries – Raspberries – Orange
Melon – Watermelon
Wheat bran (cereal) – Yogurt

To light the fire within us we need to be in control of the following negative emotions: anger, envy (including lust-sexual or otherwise), jealousy, revenge, and rage. And we need to be free from the forerunners of fear (worry, doubt, uncertainty).

The fears that hamper us the most are:
1. Fear of not being liked/accepted
2. Fear of looking foolish
3. Fear of expression, public speaking
4. Fear of making a mistake
5. Fear of not knowing the answer
6. Fear of not being perfect

7. Fear what others will say about us
8. Fear of criticism
9. Fear of growing old
10. Fear of financial loss or ruin
11. Fear of poverty
12. Fear of forgetting, not remembering
13. Fear of being alone, lack of self-acceptance
14. Fear of death, loss of power/control
15. Fear of failure, causes apathy, pessimism
16. Fear of success, inability to accept one's good
17. Fear of silence, so one chatter incessantly
18. Fear of the worst outcome, gloom, doom, unknown
19. Fear of happiness, uneasy when things going well
20. Fear of tranquility, one look for confusion/chaos

Soft Power Words™ such as: Would You, Could You, and Please, help people hear you. They are the bridge between communicating with others and managing your fear. Fear is to motivation what water is to fire. Fear will snuff out all your motivation quicker than you can rebuild it. Like water, fear is a part of life. The key is to keep fear, like water, under control. You manage your fears to Light The Fire Within You™. To do this you move through your fears one at a time. It takes action and faith to cure fear. You use the negative energy of fear in a positive way.

Our faith is developed through the practice of prayer, meditation, or spiritual mind treatment. The use of all three works to keep you in a state of positive expectancy of good. When we pray, we center our thoughts on God to acknowledge the presence of God in the situation. This helps to release your feelings of doubt, worry, anxiety and fear. These emotions only control us when we turn our attention to them. We give them power through our attention. Wherever the energy goes, power flows.

WORDS OF INSPIRATION

A Prayer

*Dear Lord! Could you ease up a bit on this load that I
must bear? I don't like my face without a smile and fur -
rowed deep with care.*

*I seemed to have lost my jaunty pace, The ready joke, and
jest; Plus the tendency to take in stride, The bad things
with the best.*

This world's hard enough as it is,
I don't want to add my bit;
I would far prefer to wear a smile
And give cheer — not woe to it.
There are already those who take delight
In painting all things dark.
They see kindling piled in little heaps
But they won't provide the spark.

I don't want special favors, Lord.
There are folks worse off than me.
But I've given others a helping hand
And I hope that you'll help me.
I do not want my burdens gone
I don't want to lie down or sit,
I only ask one favor, Lord —
Could you ease up on the load a bit?

ANON

Thing You Can Do Daily
To Light The Fire Within You

1. Avoid toxic, aggressive persons; they are a vexation to your spirit.
2. Do not allow anyone to steal your joy. People can only upset us when we allow them to do so by giving our attention to things they say or do.
3. Limit the amount of time daily you spend with angry, hostile, aggressive persons. They are toxic and poisonous.
4. Believe in a power greater than yourself. I call this power God. It has been referred to as a Higher power, Jehovah, it is nonhuman; it does not have human emotions such as sadness, depression etc. Jesus said, "Seek ye first the kingdom of God, and His righteousness and all things will be added unto you"
5. Accept that you were made in the image and likeness of God. God sees and works through us as a Spirit..
6. You are divine, take a step up in your consciousness and begin to act like the person you are.
7. When you find someone who wants to help you look at your faults, listen to their suggestions, but realize that the only person who can change you is you. It is best to perfect yourself, and allow others to do the same for themselves.
8. Get any criticism others would have you know, in writing. Then keep what is relevant and let go of what does not apply to you.
9. Give your energy and attention where it is wanted. Never force yourself on another person. But give without thought of compensation.
10. Reach out to the downtrodden, homeless, and those low in spirit and in hope. Give them your love and

compassion. Teach them to have hope, how to survive and believe in themselves. This is how you teach them to fish rather than give them a fish.

11. Give up the need to struggle. Instead trust God to know the answer. A right solution will be provided to all of your problems. All your needs will be supplied You only need unshakable faith the size of a mustard seed. Give up the need to be right. Give up the need to be perfect. Give up the belief that you are in control of things.

12. Believe in yourself. You are one of a kind. The gifts you have to share with the world can only be given by you, and no one else.

13. Be aware of the ***producers of light***; they are: choice, hopefulness, helpfulness, possibilities, powerfulness, change and cheerfulness.

The best way to spread fire to new places is to commu - nicate, to motivate yourself and others with a heart to heart connection using Soft Power Negotiation Skills ™ and words. Use Soft Power Words™ to connect with others, or communicate non-verbally to avoid power/control issues. This allows you to be in control of the emotions of anger, jealousy, envy, resentment, and hate. All blow out the light within Light depleting behavior and behaviors are: hopelessness, helplessness, powerlessness, no options, no chance, no change, no choice, and a sour disposition.

To achieve complete mastery of your negative emotions, follow the prescription in Matthew 5:44, "1 say to you, love your enemies, bless them that curse you, do good to them that hate you, and pray for them who despitefully use and persecute you. " You cannot control the action of another person. you are in control only of you. So decide how you will act or react. If the actions of others cause you to sin (make a mistake), it is best to limit your contact with them, as you learn how to be in the world, but not of it. It will require you to be in control of your emotions, attitude, behavior, mental faculties, and spiritual principles. You become the guru and attain your Christhood, the mission for us all. It matters not how far away this goal seem; start today. The journey of a thousand miles begins with one step at a time. It is a sure way to a happy day.

A Sure Way To A Happy Day

Happiness is something we create in our mind,
It's not something we search for and so seldom find
It's just waking up and beginning the day
By counting our blessings and kneeling to pray
It's giving up thoughts that breed discontent
And accepting what comes as a "gift heaven sent"
It's giving up wishing for things we have not
And making the best of whatever we've got
It's for us to know that life is determined for us,
And pursuing our tasks without fret, fume, or fuss
For it's by completing what God gives us to do
That we find real contentment and happiness, too.

HELEN STEINER RICE

To find out what motivates others, you will need to know what motivates you. A quick way to do this for yourself is to take an 8 1/2 x 11 sheet of paper and write at the top "Things I Feel Passionate About." Now list the things you feel passionate about. Write a small "p" by the ones that are personal and a large "P" by the ones you consider professional.

Things I Feel Passionate About

1.
2.
3.

AFFIRMATIONS FOR HEALTH AND WEALTH

I deny that the sins and omissions of my ancestors can influence me in any way.

Selfishness, envy, malice, jealousy, pride, anger, arrogance, cruelty, hypocrisy, obstinacy, and revenge are no part of my present understanding, and I deny all such beliefs in the race, in those with whom I associate, and in my own mind.

Plenty and Prosperity are mine by my inheritance from God, and by my steady, persistent word I now bring them into manifestation.

I deny that I inherit any belief, that in any way limits me in health, virtue, intelligence, or power to do good.

I accept that God is able to provide adequate living arrangements for me.

I am an independent person, able to provide for myself, with God's help. God is guiding me now.

I have all the money and provisions I need, available to me now. God is with me.

Chapter 10

THINGS THAT BLOCK THE FIRE WITHIN YOU: LOVE, THE HEALING BALM

Our state of mind and emotions affect our state of health, energy level, and amount of available energy to engage in life with vim, vigor, joy, and enthusiasm. If our mental state is preoccupied with worry, doubt, anger, hate, or negative, warped thinking, we are likely to experience both physical and mental fatigue. The way we think and feel about ourselves is critical to how much energy, aliveness, and joy we experience daily. We must learn to love ourselves unconditionally as we are. Love is the greatest healing power in the universe. Because God is love, when we love ourselves, we focus the power of God upon us. Therefore self love is a powerful, healing energy for our body, mind, and affairs. Love is invisible in its essence but apparent through its action.

There is nothing more detrimental to our emotional health, physical health, and spiritual health, than worry, anger, fear and hate. When we hate ourselves, disrespect ourselves, hold ourselves in contempt, have low self-worth, or low self-esteem, it affects our total being. Love is the healing balm. Love overcomes both hate and fear through the subtle power of transformation, transmutation, and sublimation.

We must learn to forgive ourselves for any mistakes we unknowingly have made in the past, against ourselves or others. The things that block the fire within you are negative behaviors, emotions, and attitudes.

118

The Three Cs are:
1. **Criticism** — tears down rather than builds up
2. **Condemnation** — to prejudge a person
3. **Complaining** — to find fault, accuse

Anger is a valuable signal, because it lets us know when something is wrong and needs to be corrected. The critical factor is whether your expression of anger is adding to the problem rather than solving it. Often when we are angry, one or more of these things are going on:

1. We want something and are not getting it.
2. From past experience, we expect trouble.
3. We feel powerless to get what we want.

Anger can lead to:
1. Angrily lashing out→Makes the situation worse
2. Hold feelings inside→Creates resentment, physical symptoms OR
You can identify the problem to handle or solve it. You do this by changing the thought you think. This is helpful when thinking about something that irritates you and makes you angry.
The premise of anger management techniques is to use your anger as a signal to identify your problem and deal with it. This, rather than act upon your anger by lashing out, to make the situation worse, or to hold your angry feelings inside.

Basic Concepts To Understand About Anger
1. Anger is an emotion
2. Reason is not employed when we are angry.
3. Anger is the results of jumping to conclusions about an outcome.
4. Anger creates a sense of energy, excitement, negative aliveness.

5. Anger is self serving.
6. Anger is addictive.
7. Anger is about power and control.
8. Anger is used to intimidate, instill fear, and as an outlet to get rid of one's inner poison/toxins.
9. You do not have a license to hurt or abuse another with your anger.
10. No one has given you permission to hurt someone because of your inability to handle your problems
11. When you are angry, you are out of control, not other person.
12. Others may provoke you to anger, but you do not have to respond angrily. When you respond as others want, they have the power to control you.
13. No one is the cause of you responding angrily. You have freedom of choice.
14. When you get angry, you are exercising power or seeking to avenge yourself.
14. You get some pleasure from hurting others, if you get angry repeatedly.
15. If you get angry repeatedly, you are unable to control your feelings of anger.
16. Are you in control of your anger or does it control you?

The basis of anger management techniques is for you to use your anger as a signal to identify your problems and deal with them. Rather than act upon your anger by lashing out, to make the situation worse, or keep your feelings of anger inside.

Write how you feel when you are angry.

Anger is an aliveness with the spirit of God or is it an addictive self seeking energy gratification.

Draw how you look when you are on fire with Divine energy that is peaceful, kind and considerate.

Anger corrodes and impedes the channels through which help can come. It disturbs the physical and mental atmosphere around us and blocks our ability to reason. Also, it prevents us from having a calm outlook and a calm resolve of mind. It is a shadow that has no real basis for existence. Love is the healing balm. A perfect love casts out anger. Love is more than a recitation of words, giving candy, flowers, or special favors.

When we love, we accept others as they are, ourselves icluded. We have peace of mind and assurance that in spite of our daily troubles, there is a force for Good in the universe (God) who sustains as we move through our fears. "God is love, and anyone who lives in love lives in God, and God is living in him. For though we have never yet seen God, when we love each other, God lives in us and his love within us grows strong." When we live by these principles we can one day say, fear came by to visit, love answered the door, and no one was there. Fear destroys the light and joy inside you. Love Is The Only Answer.

Love is patient and kind. Love is not jealous or boastful; it is not arrogant or rude. Love does not insist on its own way; it is not irritable or resentful; it does not rejoice at wrong, but rejoice in the right.

No person's life is without obstacles, problems or set-backs. We cannot always avoid obstacles. It is not important to live without problems. It is how we respond to and cope with life's problems that makes the difference. When life give you lemons, can you make lemonade out of it; or do you give up, act helpless, become hopeless, and unable to face life each day. It is how we face and overcome the obstacles in our path that makes the difference.

To feel alive, practice daily visualizing and affirming light. Say to yourself —I am light. I am love. I am willing to move through my anger to light the fire within me. I am willing to make the changes and take the steps necessary to feel and be more alive.

When we light the fire within us, we are full of energy and vitality. We move through the obstacles in our lives with ease, peace of mind and self confidence that God is working things out for our highest good and the good of all concerned. To Know and accept this allows us to **let go of the problem and let God take over;** Love, trust, and know that the God that keeps the stars in order is capable of handling your *small problem.* Love yourself enough to trust; trust God enough to let go so God can help you. Learn to embrace God rather than your problem. The more you dwell on and think about your problems, the more difficult it will be to divorce yourself from them.

Worry and distrust are like the dark; they block out our sunlight, and our joy. When we light the fire within us, lethargy, procrastination, and inaction are things of the past. We know who we are, where we are going, and why we were created. None of us knows how much time we have to complete the task we were sent here to accomplish. Each of us has been chosen and each has a different job to do, and gift to share. No one has your unique gifts. So if you do not accomplish what you were sent to do, it will not get done.

To accomplish anything, you need desire (dream) to create the vision. Your vision, when focused, will generate energy, drive, stamina, enthusiasm, and aliveness. Your aliveness is your light. It gives you energy. When you are alive and on fire with your dreams and goals you can't be stopped. Energy surges through you like electricity. You are alive and on fire with your dreams and daily tasks of life. Say often, "I am alive and I am on fire."

Affirm Daily:
I am free from fear, anxiety, worry, and uncertainty.
I have faith in God. I trust God to protect me, provide for me, and bring my affairs into divine order. This is done, right now and I give thanks.

Write what you feel is blocking the fire, enthusiasm within you. Is it apathy, boredom, have you seen it all and done it all? Have you given up on life or yourself? Express your thoughts on this topic now.

Do you tell yourself you are too old, too young, stupid, dumb, slow, tired? Close your eyes for one minute and notice what thoughts are running through your mind.

Were they uplifting, loving kind thoughts or were they negative self defeating thoughts? You may be your worst enemy, if so decide today to change your thoughts. Say to yourself I will take following corrective action today, this hour.

1.

2.

Affirm to Yourself Daily and Hourly if needed:
I Am Alive And I Am On Fire With My Dreams, Goals, And Aspirations. I can do it! I will do it.. Shalom/ Peace Today I know that I am the light that God shines through. Outer events and routine do not rule my life. Today I will do something different.

The word "enthusiasm comes from the Greek, 'en' meaning in, and 'theos' meaning God. Enthusiasm is the God within me coming out of me. I will sing unto the Lord as long as I live: I will sing praise to my God while I am alive.

Today I will let my friends know how precious they are. Today whether my family is near or far, I'll make them beautifully aware of my love.
Today I know that the time is now to be happy.
DOLLY SEWELL, NOTTINGHAM, ENGLAND

Things that take away your light and fire within are: To repeatedly dwell on negative thoughts, people, negative situations, despair, hopeless, helpless feelings, discouragement, feelings of disappointment, apathy, boredom, gloomy/doom outlook, prolonged sadness or grief.

Yesterday is a canceled check. Tomorrow is a promissory note. All we have is today. Daily Light the Fire Within You. It is your joy, it is your warmth, it is your smile, it is your energy, it is your compassion, it is your understanding, it is your love. You are the light. Let your light so shine before others, that they may see your good works and glorify God.

To Light the Fire Within You Daily:
Be Caring
Be Courteous
Be Confident
Be Capable
Be Competent
Show Compassion
Be Cooperative
Be Joyful
Be Hopeful/Be Optimistic
Be Peaceful
Be Obedient
Be Enthusiastic
Be Loving/Be Gentle with Yourself
Be Gentle With Others

IT'S A SPECIAL DAY
Something is occurring, something new is stirring
Something of the spirit, blesses me today.
Energies are swarming, totally transforming,
Something of the spirit blesses me with light.
Knowledge is provided, I am being guided,
Something of the spirit blesses me with light.
I have perfect leading to the good I'm needing,
Something of the spirit blesses me with light.
I accept my blessing; through it I am expressing,
Something of the spirit gloriously good.
Every trouble ceases; all my joy increases
Something of the spirit blesses me with good.
It's a special day; It's a special day,
I can feel it deeply in a special way
It's a special day, It's a special day,
I can feel it deeply in a special way.
WARREN MEYER/GEORGE A MINOR

BIBLIOGRAPHY

1. Holy Bible, King James Version

2. Taliferro William M., "Dealing With Fear," Creative Thought Magazine, (August 1984).

3. Guthrie E.R., The Psychology of Learning, Revised Edition, (Gloucester: Peter Smith, 1960).

4. Holy Bible, King James Version, "Dictionary Concordance," (Nashville-Camden, New York: Thomas Nelson Publishers),

5. The Living Bible Paraphrased, Wheaton: TynDale House Publishers Inc., 1971.

TESTIMONIALS

The information in the book helped me to Say Hello to my Greatness. DEE SANFORD, (Speaker and Television Personality)

The information in the book was inspiring and insightful. TOYA HICKS

The information helped me to reenergize myself and to notice how our fears impact our life. BOBBY CARNEY

INDEX

www.ingramcontent.com/pod-product-compliance
Lightning Source LLC
Chambersburg PA
CBHW031854090426
42741CB00005B/481